THE ART OF
Afternoon Tea

THE ART OF
Afternoon Tea

Tradition, etiquette & delectable
recipes for teatime treats

RYLAND PETERS & SMALL
LONDON • NEW YORK

Designers Paul Stradling & Emily Breen
Editor Gillian Haslam
Head of Production Patricia Harrington
Creative Director Leslie Harrington
Editorial Director Julia Charles

Indexer Hilary Bird

First published in 2024 by
Ryland Peters & Small
20–21 Jockey's Fields, London
WC1R 4BW
and
341 E 11th St
New York, NY 10029

10 9 8 7 6 5 4 3 2 1

Text © Mickael Benichou, Susannah Blake,
Julian Day, Matt Follas, Liz Franklin, Victoria
Hall, Hannah Miles, Suzy Pelta, Will Torrent
and Bea Vo 2024.

Design and photography © Ryland Peters &
Small 2024 (see page 192 for full credits).
Recipe collection compiled by Julia Charles.

Printed in China.

ISBN: 978-1-78879-617-0

A CIP record for this book is available from the British Library.
US Library of Congress cataloging-in-Publication Data has been applied for.

NOTES FOR COOKS

• All spoon measurements are level unless otherwise specified.
• All eggs are medium (UK) or large (US), unless specified as large, in which case US extra-large should be used. Uncooked or partially cooked eggs should not be served to the very old, frail, young children, pregnant women or those with compromised immune systems.
• When a recipe calls for clingfilm/plastic wrap, you can substitute for beeswax wraps, silicone stretch lids or compostable baking paper for greater sustainability.
• When a recipe calls for the grated zest of citrus fruit, buy unwaxed fruit and wash well before using.
• Ovens should be preheated to the specified temperatures. If using a fan-assisted oven, adjust temperatures according to the manufacturer's instructions.

FSC
www.fsc.org

MIX
Paper | Supporting
responsible forestry
FSC® C008047

Contents

Introduction

Afternoon tea is one of life's true pleasures, whether it is a brief pause during a busy day for a slice of cake and a freshly brewed cuppa, or a full-blown three-course affair with an array of sandwiches and savouries, followed by scones with jam/jelly and cream, and a grand finale of assorted dainty cakes and pastries. While receiving an invitation to afternoon tea at a smart hotel is always a thrill, there is much pleasure to be had from hosting a tea in your own home, and this book contains all the recipes you will need to make it a success.

The first chapter explains the different types of tea available, and how to brew and serve them. This is followed by a chapter on sandwiches and savouries, with ideas for exciting new sandwich fillings and bite-sized morsels to kickstart your event.

No afternoon tea is complete without a plate of fresh-from-the-oven scones, and here you will find recipes for sweet, savoury, fruity and cheesy scones. This is followed by pages offering up a tempting array of small cakes and cookies, with new twists on old favourites and modern classics, while the section on pastries and dainties shows you how to master creations that would not look out of place in the window of a pâtisserie shop. The final chapter provides recipes for larger cakes and teatime treats so delicious you'll find it impossible to resist a second slice.

To finish the book, you'll find eight suggested afternoon tea menus, which will help you to present your guests with a tea perfectly themed for the occasion or season.

Afternoon tea is the perfect excuse to dust off your best china, polish your cake forks, use your best table linen and invite friends and family over for a relaxed and delicious afternoon. So select the recipes that tempt you most from these pages and get baking!

All about tea

We are increasingly discovering the health benefits and enjoyment to be had from drinking tea. However, the differences between types of teas can be quite confusing at first, so here is a useful outline of the main types of tea. In addition, there are the 'teas' that aren't technically teas at all, in the strictest sense of the word, in that they are not made from the leaves of Camellia sinensis *(the evergreen shrub whose leaves and buds produce traditonal tea) – they are the caffeine-free infusions of various herbs, spices or fruits, often referred to as 'tisanes'.*

TYPES OF TEA

There are six main types of tea, but within these types there is a whole host of varieties. Once you get to grips with the characteristics and flavours of the different types, you will find that an exciting new adventure has begun.

Black tea

Usually strong and earthy, black teas are fully oxidized and are produced using one of two methods. In the orthodox method, the fresh tea leaves are withered for several hours and then rolled, which releases oils that coat the surface of the still-green leaves. The leaves are left until fully oxidized and then fired to prevent them from rotting. The alternative method is a mechanical process known as CTC (crush, tear, curl) and experts believe that on the whole, teas produced using this method are of a lower grade.

Black tea is used as the base of many popular flavoured teas. Earl Grey is a blend of black tea infused with oil from the bergamot orange. English and Irish breakfast teas are based on the leaves of full-bodied black teas and India's favourite Masala Chai is a sweet and aromatic blend of black tea, milk and spices that has gained huge popularity around the world. Lapsang Souchong, Darjeeling, Assam, Ceylon and Keemun are all well-known varieties of black tea.

Green tea

Unlike black teas, green teas do not go through any form of oxidization (the chemical changes that happen after exposure to air). They can be first or second flush; using very tender buds and shoots from an early season crop or more robust from later crops. Initially they are allowed to wither in a dark place, which reduces the water content. In China, the leaves are usually then roasted and left to dry out. This process kills the enzymes in the leaves, which prevents any oxidization. In Japan, this is more commonly achieved by steaming the leaves before they are rolled and dried.

Around 80 per cent of the world's green tea comes from China, and as such the leaves have interesting names. Two popular green teas are Pi Lo Chun (which translates as 'jade snail spring') and Chun Mee (which translates as 'precious eyebrows'), both named after the shape of their leaves.

The famous gunpowder tea traditionally used in Moroccan mint tea is a green tea.

Japanese green teas, such as gyokuro and sencha are gaining in popularity around the world, and matcha green tea powder, the tea traditionally used in Japanese tea ceremonies, is now widely used to flavour ice creams, noodles and cakes.

Research has uncovered amazing health benefits related to drinking green tea. Green teas are widely considered to have anti-ageing and anti-bacterial properties. Drinking green tea on a regular basis can help to reduce levels of bad cholesterol in the body. As a natural source of antioxidants, green tea is thought to help fight cancer, and investigations have also revealed that frequent consumption of green tea can aid weight loss.

A huge variety of flavoured green teas are now available to buy. However, you may prefer to add your own natural flavourings to the tea, such as a wedge of lemon or a sprig of fresh mint leaves.

Oolong tea

Oolong teas are partially oxidized, and therefore more processed than green tea but less so than black tea. They are essentially a hybrid of green and black tea, said to have been discovered by accident when a Chinese gardener was distracted by a deer that he subsequently killed and prepared to eat, forgetting about the tea that he had been brewing prior to his sudden diversion. Returning to the tea the next day, he found the leaves had changed colour due to partial oxidization – but he carried on and finished the tea anyway. The tea's increased aroma and depth of flavour made it a favourite – and so, oolong was born.

Oolong tea falls into two different categories. For darker oolongs, the leaves are tossed in bamboo drums to start the oxidization process. When they are around 60–70 per cent oxidized, the leaves are dried. The lighter, greener oolongs are only 30 per cent oxidized and are wrapped in cloths and machine-rolled before being dried. Both types of tea have unique characteristics, and many tea aficionados believe oolongs to be the most distinctive and agreeable of all teas.

They are ideal for multiple steepings and it is said that the flavour of the tea gets better and better each time the pot is filled up. Dedicated oolong fans believe that the fourth or fifth steeping releases the best flavour – although you'd need a pretty strong bladder to get to your fifth cup without retiring.

Formosa oolong comes from Taiwan, China. Imperial formosa oolong is an especially acclaimed tea. Traditionally drunk by Taiwan's Buddhist monks, it is considered one of the best teas in the world.

Pu-erh tea

Pu-erh teas are oxidized to a similar level as green teas, but are dark in colour and unique in that they go through a process known as post-fermentation. Traditionally, pu-erh comes from the Yunnan province in China and is gaining in popularity because one of its purported health benefits is that it is believed to aid weight loss. For 'raw' pu-erh, the processed tea is compressed into cakes and left to age for up to 50 years, making it very expensive. However, 'cooked' pu-erh is increasingly produced, which takes much less time to manufacture and involves the introduction of a special bacterial culture that speeds up the maturation.

Specialist tea suppliers will sell pu-erh tea cakes and bricks. The tea must be gently prised from the cake or brick, or the leaves will be damaged, which could have a negative effect on the flavour of the tea. The best tool to use for this delicate operation is a pu-erh knife, which is a special 'tea needle' that can be lightly inserted into the brick or cake and used to work the tea loose. However, loose leaf pu-erh is widely available from tea specialists, supermarkets, department stores and even health food shops.

White tea

White tea is the least processed of all the teas and is generally the most esteemed. Only the topmost bud and leaves are picked from the bush, sometimes only the bud, and they are always first flush. The buds must be picked before they unfurl, are handled as little as possible and processed minimally. They are withered in the sunshine or, in bad weather, in a warm room. White teas are silvery in colour, have a mild flavour, are low in caffeine and have the highest antioxidant content of any of the teas.

Baihao yinzhen ('silver needle') and Pai Mutan or Bai Mudan ('white peony') are particularly good white teas to look out for. Slightly sweet and deliciously mellow, silver needle is always a good choice.

Yellow tea

Yellow tea is produced in a similar way to green tea, but the leaves are left to turn yellow before they are dried. Yellow tea is generally milder and sweeter than green tea.

This is one of the rarest types of tea and is relatively undiscovered in the west. Yellow tea has a sweet, mellow flavour and is particular to the Sichuan and Hunan provinces of China. It may take a little effort to get hold of some (try specialist tea suppliers), but as you begin to discover and enjoy the world of specialist teas, you will realize it's one worth tracking down!

Tea equipment

Strictly speaking, the only essential things needed to make tea are a receptacle of some sort (a cup, mug or heatproof glass), some form of tea and boiled water (good-quality tea leaves tend to sink, so you shouldn't be struggling with too many stray leaves).

Of course, if you're using a tea bag, you'll need something to fish the tea bag out once your tea is brewed to the desired strength. But when you discover the world of truly amazing teas that are available, making the tea itself becomes a really enjoyable part of the whole process. Pouring the tea from a beautiful pot is a delight, and filling up a favourite tea stick or tea ball or making your own-blend tea bag is a real pleasure, so there are various pieces of equipment you might like to invest in. Tea paraphernalia often also makes a great gift. Here are a few ideas you might like to consider.

Teapots

Once upon a time, a teapot was as much a piece of essential kitchen kit as the saucepan or pot. When the tea bag came along, things changed. If you think of the importance and ceremonies associated with tea around the world, it seems a shame that tea-making in the west was ever reduced to simply sticking a tea bag willy-nilly into a mug, pouring boiling water over it and squashing it with a spoon. Thankfully, proper tea is making a well deserved return to the table!

Teapots come in all shapes and sizes and a variety of materials, from the very beautiful to the practical. They become a little like a favourite mug or cup and tea will definitely taste different depending on what pot it is made in. It would

be a shame to serve a delicate white tea from the sort of traditional Brown Betty teapot that is customarily associated with a strong breakfast brew, but there is something about those sturdy teapots that makes them perfect for use on the table alongside a cooked breakfast and lots of hot buttery toast and marmalade.

Delicate white teas and green teas are perfect served in pretty china pots that reflect their delicate flavour, although glass is a great option for the flowering tea balls. Glass teapots now have better insulation, so they keep the tea hot, and it's interesting to watch tea leaves or a tea ball unfurl as the brewing process takes place.

A good choice for an everyday teapot is a sturdier earthenware pot that's a white version of the Brown Betty. Of course, in an ideal world you would have a teapot to match the type of tea you are making. There are some beautiful Asian-style teapots with handles that somehow make drinking Japanese teas a very special experience, but not all of us have the budget or the cupboard space!

A good all-purpose pot would be made from not-too-delicate china. Some people favour the teapots that come with built-in infusers, so

that the tea doesn't over-brew, but if you're worried about that, you can scoop the tea into an infuser and clip it to the side of the pot, then remove it when you're happy with the strength of the tea. Whatever the preference, there's a teapot out there for everyone.

Tea balls, tea sticks & infusers

Tea balls, tea sticks and infusers make it easy to brew loose-leaf tea while keeping the leaves contained, making them as convenient as tea bags while still allowing you to enjoy your favourite loose-leaf tea. However, some tea experts argue that they restrict the movement of the leaves and therefore don't allow the true characteristics of the tea to come out in the brewing process. They can be used in a

teapot or individual mug or cup, and come in all shapes and sizes, from the plain and practical to the ornate. They are usually made from stainless steel, although they do come in silver, for those for whom cost isn't a consideration!

Tea cosies

Just as the teapot was once a household item, so too was the tea cosy. Whether knitted, crocheted, sewn or shop bought, from the plain and practical to the entertaining and elaborate, the purpose of the tea cosy was to keep the pot warm. Sceptics argue that a tea cosy won't make much difference to keeping a pot hot, and, of course, tea left to sit could become over-brewed and bitter as the tannins continue to be released, but there is something fun and cheery about a tea cosy, so it's down to personal choice as to whether you have one (or several) in your personal *batterie de thé*!

Tea caddies

Tea caddies, or canisters, have been around for as long as tea itself, and range from the everyday to the highly decorative, but essentially they do the necessary job of keeping the tea fresh, and preserving its flavour. Premium teas can be bought in nice caddies, but are also increasingly sold in foil

packages and ideally should be transferred to an airtight container upon opening.

Strainers, squeezers & sundries

Pouring tea through a strainer into a cup does away with the risk of getting leaves in the cup and the embarrassment of trying to pick tea leaves out of your teeth. Good-quality tea leaves do sink to the bottom of the pot however, and so controlled pouring will help if you don't have a strainer to hand. They are inexpensive and easy to buy so a strainer is a good investment. Tea bag squeezers are a little bit of an indulgence, but they are a little more sophisticated than squashing the bag against the side of your cup with a spoon. There are also tea-bag tidies, measuring and caddie spoons and all kinds of bits and bobs you can add to your kit as your enjoyment of fine teas unfolds.

Helpful tea terminology

The science surrounding the harvesting, production, brewing and serving of tea, lends itself to a few pieces of jargon that you may come across when exploring the world of tea.

Fannings or **Dust** These are mainly low-quality leftover leaves that are often used in tea bags.

Flowery 'Flowery' indicates that the tea includes buds and leaves, and is also a sign of good quality.

Flush Used to describe the tree's growing season, when it is pushing out new leaves. A 'first flush' tea is produced using the first tender buds and shoots, and is considered the most delicate in taste, although second flush tea leaves are thought to have a little more body. Subsequent flushes are used but generally not acknowledged.

Grading Tea can be graded by its region of origin, such as Assam, Darjeeling, China, Ceylon (Sri Lanka) etc., but the grading of the leaves is also an important aspect of tea-making, as small leaves brew at different rates to larger leaves and produce different results.

Orange Orange pekoe teas belong in the orthodox black tea category and have a recognized grading system, with leaves classified into larger leaf grades and 'broken' leaf grades (smaller pieces). The term 'orange' supposedly dates to the East India Trading Company presenting tea to the Dutch royal family, the House of Orange, and then promoting the tea as 'orange pekoe' to imply a royal warrant.

Picking Also called 'plucking', this happens between spring and autumn/fall, the growing season in countries such as China and northern India. In countries where the weather is more consistent, picking takes place all year. The quality of the tea is determined by the number of leaves and buds plucked from each plant.

Steeping The essential process of soaking tea leaves in water. How you brew your tea is personal preference but some teas, such as oolong, are suited to multiple steepings, and often result in an enhanced, richer flavour.

Tippy The tea includes the highest proportion of buds, or 'tips', and is of the highest quality.

Bringing tea to the table

TEA-PRODUCING REGIONS

From its origins in China centuries ago, major tea cultivation has now spread to the verdant hills, high mountains and coastal regions of a handful of countries. India, Japan and Sri Lanka join China as producers of the acclaimed teas.

China

The humid tropical and sub-tropical provinces of southern China are home to the bulk of the country's tea estates. China produces so much tea that the well-known phrase 'not for all the tea in China' came about (meaning 'not at any price'), although India has now become the world's biggest producer of tea.

India

Assam and Darjeeling are often thought of types of tea, when in fact they are the regions in India in which those teas are cultivated. Darjeeling tea carries a PGi certificate, which means that only teas cultivated, produced and processed within a specified area of Darjeeling can actually carry the name. Genuine Darjeeling tea should carry the official logo, introduced by the Tea Board of India. Darjeeling teas were primarily black teas, but now green, oolong and white teas are increasingly being produced.

Japan

Tea was originally introduced to Japan from China by Buddhist monks. Nowadays, Japan is renowned for excellent green teas and the Shizuoka and Kagoshima regions are principal producers.

Sri Lanka

Formerly known as Ceylon, Sri Lanka's humidity, temperatures and rainfall all help to produce high-quality teas. Sri Lankan teas are largely black, and the Sri Lankan Board of Tea issues a quality mark to identify pure Ceylon teas.

Taiwan, China

Taiwan is an island situated off the south-eastern coast of China's mainland. Because the bushes are cultivated at comparatively low altitudes, the island produced a high percentage of oolong teas.

BREWING THE PERFECT CUPPA

Tea aficionados all around the world have argued for years about how to brew the perfect cuppa, but loose tea is generally considered to produce a better quality tea than bags. Loose teas are most often produced from the whole leaf and allow the user more control over the strength of the tea; more leaves in the pot will usually make a stronger tea. Loose-leaf tea can usually be steeped several times; some teas are even thought to benefit from it.

Real tea connoisseurs will pour an initial amount of hot water into a teapot containing the leaves, then pour the water out, rather than simply warming the pot before adding the leaves. The benefit of doing so is that any dust that is clinging to the leaves will be washed away, and the leaves are supposedly primed to swell, encouraging maximum flavour.

The Royal Society of Chemistry has published a guide to making the perfect cup of tea. They advise using freshly drawn water every time. When water boils, it loses some of its oxygen, and oxygen helps bring out the flavour of the tea. They recommend a ceramic teapot, as metal can sometimes taint the flavour of the tea.

The advice is to brew the tea for 3–4 minutes (although this would depend on the type of tea), since polyphenolic compounds (tannins) are released after this time, which give the tea its colour and some of its flavour. However, leaving the tea to infuse for longer than this apparently introduces high molecular-weight tannins, which can give the tea a bad (or bitter) aftertaste.

A MATTER OF MILK

Although many of the teas are better without milk, the subject of when to add milk to teas that can take milk is a hotly contested one. Does the milk come first? Or the tea? Well, The Royal Society of Chemistry advocates that the milk (always fresh and chilled, and never long-lasting UHT) goes into the cup first, because degradation of the milk occurs if milk encounters temperatures above 75°C (167°F). The report says that 'if milk is poured into hot tea, individual drops separate from the bulk of the milk and come into contact with the high temperatures of the tea for enough time for significant denaturation to occur'. This is much less likely to happen if hot water is added to the milk.

Once full mixing has occurred, the temperature should be below 75°C (167°F).

Apparently, the perfect temperature at which to drink tea is 60–65°C (140–149°F) 'to avoid vulgar slurping which results from drinking tea at too high a temperature.'

The author of the report also goes on to say, somewhat tongue in cheek, that 'to gain optimum ambience for enjoyment of tea, aim to achieve a seated drinking position, where quietness and calm will elevate the moment to a special dimension. For best results, carry a heavy bag of shopping – or walk the dog – in cold, driving rain for at least half an hour beforehand. This will make the tea taste out of this world.'

Hopefully by reading this chapter, you will realize that tea can taste truly wonderful without having to haul heavy bags or schlep around the stormy streets beforehand!

SETTING THE TEA TABLE

If you are serving a formal sit-down tea, make sure you provide appropriate utensils for whatever food you are offering.

You may need a butter knife, a pastry fork and even a spoon for a particularly creamy cake. These implements should all be set to the right of the plate, with the napkin placed on the left (or on top of the plate if you prefer). For a proper afternoon tea, it's imperative to use your very best teacups and saucers; mugs just won't give you the same sense of occasion.

1 Napkin in a simple fold

2 Side plate

3 Butter knife

4 Dessertspoon

5 Pastry fork

6 Saucer

7 Teacup

8 Teaspoon

Chapter 1

Sandwiches
& Savouries

Cucumber & mint sandwiches

This is a simple twist on the traditional and ever-popular cucumber sandwich, with the mint leaves adding an extra layer of flavour and freshness.

✂ — • • — ✂

6 slices of white or brown bread
whipped butter, for spreading
1 tablespoon table salt
1 cucumber
a small bunch of fresh mint
100 ml/⅓ cup crème fraîche

MAKES 12

Lay out the slices of bread on a bread board. Spread whipped butter evenly and thinly on the slices to seal the bread.

In a mixing bowl, add a few cm/inches of cold water and the table salt, then whisk to dissolve the salt. Taste the water to check it has a hint of saltiness.

Peel and thinly slice the cucumber. Place the slices into the salted water for a few minutes, then remove them and set aside.

Finely chop the mint and whisk into the crème fraîche to make a minty cream.

Spread the mint cream on three of the slices of buttered bread. Lay the cucumber slices on top of the cream and cover with the second slices of buttered bread. Cut the edges off the sandwiches, then cut them into four triangles. Serve.

Smoked salmon & dill mayonnaise sandwiches

Dill and smoked salmon are a classic combination because they are perfectly balanced. Try using hot smoked salmon for a tasty alternative.

6 slices of white or brown bread
whipped butter, for spreading
50 ml/3½ tablespoons mayonnaise
a small bunch of fresh dill, picked
    and finely chopped
200 g/7 oz. smoked salmon,
    thinly sliced

MAKES 12

Lay out the slices of bread on a bread board. Spread whipped butter evenly and thinly on the slices to seal the bread.

Spread the mayonnaise generously on three of the slices of buttered bread, then sprinkle with finely chopped dill.

Lay slices of smoked salmon, two layers thick, over the dill and mayonnaise, and cover with the second slices of buttered bread. Cut the edges off the sandwiches, then cut each into four triangles. Serve.

Aubergine & mayonnaise sandwiches

Aubergine/eggplant goes particularly well with the subtly smoky flavour of paprika, as in this sandwich filling.

1 large aubergine/eggplant
vegetable oil, for drizzling
6 slices of white or brown bread
whipped butter, for spreading
100 ml/$\frac{1}{3}$ cup mayonnaise
3 teaspoons smoked paprika
table salt

MAKES 12

Cut the aubergine/eggplant lengthways into eight thin slices and lightly season with salt. Place into a large, preheated, dry non-stick frying pan/skillet. Heat on high and allow the aubergine to cook and char a little on both sides. Drizzle a little vegetable oil over the aubergine and fry for a couple of minutes. Leave to cool.

Lay out the slices of bread on a bread board. Spread whipped butter evenly and thinly on the slices to seal the bread.

In a mixing bowl, mix together the mayonnaise and smoked paprika. Spread the mayonnaise evenly on three of the slices of buttered bread. Slice the cooked aubergine into 2.5-cm/1-inch strips and place these on the mayonnaise, overlapping them to make a generous layer of aubergine. Cover with the second slices of buttered bread. Cut the edges off the sandwiches, then cut each into four triangles. Serve.

Hummus & rocket sandwiches

Rocket/arugula leaves to add a little peppery heat and freshness to the hummus in this sandwich.

———— • • • ————

6 slices of white or brown bread

whipped butter, for spreading

bag of wild rocket/arugula, washed

HUMMUS

200 g/1½ cups drained cooked chickpeas/garbanzo beans

grated zest and freshly squeezed juice of 1 lemon

50 g/2 oz. tahini

1 garlic clove

1 teaspoon ground cumin

1 teaspoon smoked paprika

½ teaspoon table salt

a splash of extra-virgin olive oil

MAKES 12

For the hummus, put all of the ingredients into a small food processor and blitz for about a minute, until it forms a rough paste. Add a little more oil, if needed, to thin the mixture. Leave for at least 30 minutes for the flavours to infuse before serving.

Lay out the slices of bread on a bread board. Spread whipped butter evenly and thinly on the slices to seal the bread.

Spread the hummus generously on three of the slices of bread, then cover each with at least three layers of washed rocket/arugula leaves. Cover with the second slices of buttered bread. Cut the edges off the sandwiches, then cut each into four triangles. Serve.

(Pictured opposite)

Beef & horseradish sandwiches

Experts claim traditional roast beef sandwich should be served rare, but it's what you like that counts, so cook the beef to your preferred level. This sandwich is an excellent way to use up the leftovers from the Sunday roast, with horseradish sauce adding a little fire.

———— ⚬ • • ⚬ ————

6 slices of white or brown bread
whipped butter, for spreading
100 g/3½ oz. horseradish sauce
250 g/9 oz. thinly sliced cold
    roast beef

MAKES 12

Lay out the slices of bread on a bread board. Spread whipped butter evenly and thinly on the slices to seal the bread.

Spread a thin layer of horseradish sauce on three of the slices of buttered bread (or spread more generously if you like your beef extra spicy).

Lay slices of the beef on top, ideally at least three thin slices deep. Cover with the second slices of buttered bread. Cut the edges off the sandwiches, then cut each into four triangles. Serve.

Egg & cress sandwiches

This sandwich filling is another true classic, and one many of us will remember from our childhood. Seven minutes in boiling water (for a room-temperature egg) gives a just-hard-boiled/-cooked egg perfect for this recipe. If you prefer to add mayonnaise to the eggs, see the recipe on page 34.

6 slices of white or brown bread
whipped butter, for spreading
2 cold hard-boiled/hard-cooked
   eggs
a pinch of ground white pepper
a pinch of table salt
30 g/1 oz. cress

MAKES 9

Lay out the slices of bread on a bread board. Spread whipped butter evenly and thinly on the slices to seal the bread.

Peel the eggs and place in a mixing bowl. Mash the eggs with a fork, adding a generous pinch of white pepper and salt.

Spread the mashed egg mixture on three of the slices of buttered bread, then sprinkle with an even covering of fresh cress. Cover with the second slices of buttered bread. Cut the edges off the sandwiches, then cut each into three fingers. Serve.

(Pictured on previous page)

Coronation chicken sandwiches

This is a fresh take on the classic coronation chicken re-invented in 1953 to celebrate Queen Elizabeth II's coronation. The original dish was made with mayonnaise and curry powder, but here we use some classic, fresh, individual spices.

6 slices of white or brown bread
whipped butter, for spreading
1 teaspoon coriander seeds
½ teaspoon ground turmeric
½ teaspoon chilli/chili powder
½ teaspoon fenugreek powder
a pinch of ground cumin
150 ml/⅔ cup fresh mayonnaise
300 g/10½ oz. cold cooked chicken, finely diced

MAKES 12

Lay out the slices of bread on a bread board. Spread whipped butter evenly and thinly on the slices to seal the bread.

In a dry frying pan/skillet, heat the coriander seeds until they start to crack and pop. Take the pan off the heat and add all the other spices, mixing with a wooden spoon and using the residual heat to cook them. Crush the coriander seeds with the back of the wooden spoon.

Place the mayonnaise in a mixing bowl and add the spices. Mix to combine evenly, then add the chicken. Fold the meat through the mixture to coat it evenly.

Spread the coronation chicken generously on three of the slices of bread and cover each with the second slices of buttered bread. Cut the edges off the sandwiches, then cut each into four triangles. Serve.

Ham & mustard sandwiches

The simplicity of this sandwich means the ingredients need to be of the best quality. A good cured ham is vastly different from a cheap pressed ham. For a proper afternoon tea, the ham should be wafer thin.

6 slices of white or brown bread
whipped butter, for spreading
English mustard, to taste
300 g/10½ oz. cured ham,
    thinly sliced

MAKES 12

Lay out the slices of bread on a bread board. Spread whipped butter evenly and thinly on the slices to seal the bread.

Spread about half a teaspoon of English mustard (or to taste) on three of the slices of bread. Divide the ham between the three slices and then cover each with the second slices of buttered bread. Cut the edges off the sandwiches, then cut each into four triangles. Serve.

Finger sandwich selection

Afternoon tea just isn't afternoon tea without a plate of elegant sandwiches, cut into slim fingers. Here are two innovative fillings, plus one true classic.

12 thin slices of white or brown bread
whipped butter, for spreading
salt and freshly ground black pepper

PARMA HAM & FIG FILLING
40 g/1½ oz. thinly sliced Parma ham
1 ripe fig
½ teaspoon balsamic vinegar
½ teaspoon olive oil
a handful of rocket/arugula leaves

EGG MAYONNAISE FILLING
2 tablespoons good-quality mayonnaise
½ teaspoon grated lemon zest
2 cold hard-boiled/hard-cooked, peeled and chopped
a handful of cress

STILTON & PEAR FILLING
50 g/2 oz. Stilton cheese, thinly sliced
1 pear

MAKES 18

Lay out the slices of bread on a bread board. Spread whipped butter evenly and thinly on the slices to seal the bread.

To make the Parma ham and fig sandwiches, fold the ham on top of two slices of the bread. Cut the fig into thin wedges, remove and discard the skin, then arrange the wedges on top of the ham. Whisk the vinegar and olive oil together in a small bowl, season with salt and pepper and drizzle over the fig. Scatter rocket/arugula leaves on top, then top with another two slices of buttered bread.

To make the egg mayonnaise sandwiches, combine the mayonnaise and lemon zest and season with black pepper. Add the chopped eggs and fold together. Divide the mixture between two slices of the bread and spread out evenly. Top with cress and another two slices of buttered bread.

To make the Stilton and pear sandwiches, arrange the Stilton

over two slices of the bread. Slice the pear into thin wedges, remove and discard the core, then arrange the pear wedges on top of the cheese. Season with black pepper, then top with another two slices of buttered bread.

To cut the sandwiches, lay your hand on top of the sandwich and press down gently. Using a sharp serrated knife and a gentle sawing motion, cut off the crusts. Next, cut the sandwich lengthways into three fingers. Serve.

Welsh rarebit

This is the ultimate cheese on toast, with a hot, cheesy, ale-infused béchamel sauce under a crispy cheese topping.

⊰ • • • ⊱

BÉCHAMEL

40 g/3 tablespoons butter

25 g/3 tablespoons plain/
    all-purpose flour

100 ml/$\frac{1}{3}$ cup full-fat/whole milk

300 ml/$1\frac{1}{4}$ cups ale

Worcestershire sauce

1 teaspoon English mustard

150 g/2 cups grated/shredded
    Parmesan cheese

150 g/$1\frac{2}{3}$ cups grated/shredded
    Cheddar cheese

table salt, to taste

TOAST

1 ciabatta roll, thinly sliced

vegetable oil

TOPPING

50 g/generous $\frac{1}{2}$ cup grated/
    shredded Parmesan cheese

50 g/$\frac{1}{2}$ cup grated/shredded
    Cheddar cheese

MAKES 12

For the béchamel, in a small saucepan, heat the butter and flour over a medium heat. Leave on the heat until the butter is foaming, then whisk the mixture to a smooth paste. With the pan still on the heat, add all the milk and whisk until thoroughly combined. Slowly add the ale, whisking to make a light brown sauce with a cream-like consistency.

Add a few glugs of Worcestershire sauce and the mustard, then add both cheeses. Whisk over a low heat until a cheesy, ale-infused, béchamel sauce is formed. Add a generous pinch of salt to taste. Add a little more Worcestershire sauce and mustard if you prefer a stronger flavour.

It is easier to use the sauce when chilled, so make it in advance if you can and refrigerate. The sauce will keep for several days in the fridge. The recipe makes more than you need for one batch of Welsh Rarebit so you can freeze what you won't use this time.

Preheat the oven to 140°C fan/
160°C/325°F/Gas 3.

For the toast, drizzle the ciabatta
slices with a little oil. Place on
a baking sheet and bake in the
preheated oven for 5 minutes,
until browned and crispy.

To finish, spread a generous
portion of the béchamel sauce on
each piece of toast, then scatter
with the mixed topping cheeses.
Bake in the preheated oven until
golden brown on top; 5–7 minutes
should do it. Serve warm.

Little toasts with anchovy butter & quails' eggs

Often referred to as Gentleman's Relish, there's something quintessentially English about anchovy relish spread on crisp little toasts. These sophisticated bites make a wonderful start to afternoon tea, especially when served with a light, refreshing cup of Earl Grey or Darjeeling. Leftover relish can be stored in the fridge for several days.

$\sim$ • • $\sim$

50 g/3 oz. canned anchovy fillets, about 8, drained

60 ml/¼ cup full-fat/whole milk

60 g/4 tablespoons unsalted butter

a pinch of cayenne pepper

a pinch of ground nutmeg

a pinch of ground coriander

¼ teaspoon freshly squeezed lemon juice

8 quails' eggs

4 wafer-thin slices of brown bread

2–3 tablespoons freshly chopped flat-leaf parsley

freshly ground black pepper

MAKES 16

Soak the anchovy fillets in the milk for about 10 minutes.

Drain the anchovy fillets and put them in a food processor with the butter, cayenne pepper, nutmeg, coriander, lemon juice and a good grinding of black pepper. Process until smooth and creamy.

Bring a saucepan of water to the boil, add the quails' eggs, then reduce the heat and simmer for about 4 minutes. Drain, then cover in cold water and let cool.

To serve, peel the eggs and cut in half lengthways. Toast the slices of bread until crisp and golden. Cut off and discard the crusts, then cut into quarters. Spread with a thin layer of anchovy relish, top with half a quail's egg and sprinkle with a little parsley. Serve immediately.

Smoked salmon
& asparagus crostini

Topped with a zesty lemon mayonnaise, smoked salmon and asparagus tips, these crisp little crostini add a delicious twist to the more traditional smoked salmon sandwich.

1 small baguette

12 asparagus tips

$2\frac{1}{2}$ tablespoons good-quality mayonnaise

$\frac{3}{4}$ teaspoon grated lemon zest

6–7 drops of Tabasco sauce

75 g/$2\frac{1}{2}$ oz. smoked salmon, cut into 12 strips

$\frac{1}{2}$ lemon, for squeezing

freshly ground black pepper

olive oil, for brushing

MAKES 12

Preheat the oven to 170°C fan/ 190°C/375°F/Gas 5.

Cut 12 thin slices of baguette on the diagonal, about 1 cm/$\frac{1}{2}$ inch thick, and brush both sides with olive oil. Place on a baking sheet and bake in the preheated oven for about 10 minutes until crisp and golden. Transfer to a wire rack to cool.

Pour about 2 cm/1 inch water into a frying pan/skillet and bring to the boil. Add the asparagus tips and simmer gently for 3–4 minutes until just tender. Drain, refresh under cold water, then pat dry with kitchen paper.

Combine the mayonnaise, lemon zest and Tabasco sauce. Spoon a dollop of the mayonnaise onto each crostini, then top with a strip of smoked salmon and an asparagus tip. Squeeze over a little lemon juice, grind over a little black pepper and serve immediately.

Baby rarebits with beetroot & orange relish

Topped with jewel-coloured beetroot/beet relish, these baby rarebits make a pretty addition to the tea table.

1 small baguette

3 tablespoons white wine

100 g/3½ oz. mature/very sharp Cheddar cheese, grated (you need a well-flavoured cheese for this recipe)

1 teaspoon Dijon mustard

2 egg yolks

freshly ground black pepper

fresh dill sprigs, to garnish

BEETROOT & ORANGE RELISH

1 tablespoon olive oil

1 shallot, finely chopped

1 teaspoon grated fresh ginger

seeds of 2 cardamom pods, crushed

1 beetroot/beet, peeled and grated

¼ cooking apple, peeled, cored and grated

freshly squeezed juice of 1 orange

salt and freshly ground black pepper

MAKES 12

To make the relish, heat the olive oil in a frying pan/skillet and gently fry the shallot for about 3 minutes. Add the ginger and cardamom seeds and fry for another minute. Add the beetroot/beet, apple and orange juice, and season well with salt and pepper. Cook very gently, stirring frequently, for about 20 minutes until tender and moist, but not wet. Check and adjust the seasoning, if necessary, then set aside.

Cut 12 thin slices of baguette on the diagonal, about 1 cm/½ inch thick.

Put the wine, cheese and mustard in a small saucepan and heat gently, until the cheese has melted. Season with black pepper, beat in the egg yolks and set aside.

Grill/broil the slices of baguette on one side until golden. Turn over, spoon on the cheese mixture and grill for another 2–3 minutes until golden and bubbling. Top with the relish, sprinkle with dill sprigs and serve immediately.

Olive & anchovy whirls

These cute little pinwheels take their inspiration from two popular savoury canapés: palmiers and anchovy straws.

70 g/¾ cup pitted/stoned black olives

30 g/1 oz. anchovy fillets in olive oil, chopped

1 garlic clove, crushed

1 tablespoon finely chopped fresh parsley

1–2 tablespoons olive oil

500 g/1 lb. 2 oz. all-butter puff pastry/dough, thawed if frozen

flour, for dusting

freshly ground black pepper

2 baking sheets, lined with parchment paper

MAKES ABOUT 40

Tip the olives, anchovies, garlic, parsley and a good grinding of black pepper into the bowl of a food processor. Add a little of the olive oil and blend until finely chopped and almost the consistency of a paste – you may not need all of the olive oil.

Cut the block of pastry in half – you will find it easier to work with two smaller pieces rather than one large piece. Roll out one piece on a lightly floured work surface into a 40 x 20 cm/16 x 8 inches rectangle.

Using a palette knife, spread half of the olive paste in a smooth layer over the pastry and trim the edges of the pastry. Starting at one of the shorter (20-cm/8-inch) ends, roll the pastry into a tight spiral with the paste inside. Wrap in clingfilm/plastic wrap and repeat with the second piece of pastry and remaining olive paste.

Put the rolls in the freezer for about 2 hours until firm.

Preheat the oven to 170°C fan/190°C/375°F/Gas 5.

Slice each pastry log into discs about 5 mm/¼ inch thick and arrange on the prepared baking sheets, leaving a little space between each one. Bake on the middle shelf of the preheated oven for about 20 minutes or until crisp and golden brown.

Serve warm from the oven.

Crab mayonnaise éclairs

These bite-sized savoury spiced éclairs encase beautifully picked white crab meat, with a little lemon and mustard mayonnaise finished off with some peppery rocket/arugula.

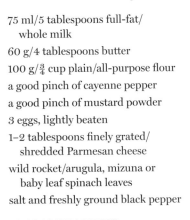

75 ml/5 tablespoons full-fat/
    whole milk

60 g/4 tablespoons butter

100 g/¾ cup plain/all-purpose flour

a good pinch of cayenne pepper

a good pinch of mustard powder

3 eggs, lightly beaten

1–2 tablespoons finely grated/
    shredded Parmesan cheese

wild rocket/arugula, mizuna or
    baby leaf spinach leaves

salt and freshly ground black pepper

CRAB MAYONNAISE

4 tablespoons good-quality
    mayonnaise

zest and juice of ½ lemon

½–1 teaspoon Dijon mustard

a pinch of cayenne pepper

250 g/8 oz. white crab meat

a large piping/pastry bag fitted with
    a 1-cm/⅜-inch plain nozzle/tip

2 baking sheets, lined with
    parchment paper

MAKES ABOUT 30

Preheat the oven to 160°C fan/
180°C/350°F/Gas 4.

Put 75 ml/5 tablespoons water in a medium saucepan with the milk and butter and set over a medium heat. Stir constantly to melt the butter. As soon as the mixture comes to the boil, reduce the heat slightly and, working quickly and keeping the pan over a low heat, stir in the flour, cayenne pepper and mustard powder. Season well with salt and black pepper. Beat vigorously until the mixture is smooth and cleanly leaves the sides of the pan – this will take about 2 minutes.

Transfer the dough to a stand mixer or mixing bowl using a handheld electric whisk and gradually beat in the eggs 1 tablespoon at a time. You might not need all of the egg – when the dough is soft and smooth and drops off a spoon leaving a 'V' shape behind, it is ready.

Scoop the dough into the piping/ pastry bag and pipe 30 éclair buns onto the prepared baking sheets, leaving plenty of space between each one. Scatter with grated Parmesan cheese and bake on the middle shelves of the preheated oven for 10–15 minutes until well risen, golden brown and sound hollow in the middle when tapped.

Remove from the oven and make a small hole in the side of each bun with a skewer. Return to the oven for a further 1 minute to dry out the insides. Leave to cool on a wire rack until completely cold.

To make the crab mayonnaise, spoon the mayonnaise into a bowl, add the lemon zest and juice, mustard, cayenne pepper and a good seasoning of salt and black pepper. Mix to combine and taste. Add more salt and black pepper if required, then add the crab meat and stir gently to coat.

Using a serrated knife split the éclairs in half, lay wild rocket/ arugula, mizuna or baby spinach leaves in the bottom of each bun and top with a heaped teaspoonful of crab mayonnaise. Top with the lids and serve.

Chapter 2
Scones

Plain scones

Plain scones are anything but! They are light, buttery, melt in the mouth, perfectly complemented by homemade jam. You have achieved perfect scones when they form a natural crack around the middle when baked, so you can pull them in two. Be careful not to overwork the dough or they will not rise.

500 g/3¾ cups self-raising/rising flour, plus extra for dusting

100 g/7 tablespoons butter, chilled

30 g/2½ tablespoons caster/granulated sugar

100 ml/⅓ cup full-fat/whole milk

100 ml/⅓ cup double/heavy cream

1 egg yolk

a 7.5-cm/3-inch round cookie cutter

a baking sheet, lined with parchment paper

MAKES 8

• • •

Preheat the oven to 200°C fan/220°C/425°F/Gas 7.

Add the flour, butter in small pieces (about 20 g/1½ tablespoons each) and the sugar to a food processor and pulse until they form a crumb.

Continue pulsing the mixture whilst adding the milk, then the cream in a steady stream, until the mixture forms a dough ball that just holds together.

Lightly flour your hands and a cool, flat surface (marble is ideal). Press the dough out to about a thickness of 5 cm/2 inches. Use the cookie cutter to cut out the scones. Re-press the leftover dough together to maximize the number of scones, but always use the cutter to form sharp edges or the scones will not rise properly. Place on the lined baking sheet.

Make a glaze by whisking the egg yolk and brush the tops of each round with the glaze.

Bake in the preheated oven for 12–14 minutes until just cooked through and risen. If you wish, carefully split one scone to check the centre is cooked.

Scones are best eaten on the day of baking.

Fruited scones

This is the classic fruited scone, a staple on afternoon tea menus for as long as afternoon tea has been an event. This recipe uses dark raisins, but sultanas/golden raisins would also work well. Serve with the traditional accompaniments of a fruity, berry-laden jam or jelly and thick, luscious clotted cream (and enjoy the inevitable debate on whether to add the jam or cream first!).

400 g/3 cups strong/bread flour, plus extra for dusting

60 g/scant ⅓ cup caster/granulated sugar

30 g/3 tablespoons baking powder

a small pinch of salt

60 g/½ stick butter

250 ml/1 cup buttermilk

100 g/¾ cup (dark) raisins

1 beaten egg, for glazing

TO SERVE

good-quality jam/jelly of your choosing

clotted cream

a 5-cm/2-inch round cookie cutter

a baking sheet, lined with parchment paper

MAKES ABOUT 24

Put the flour, sugar, baking powder, salt and butter in a mixing bowl. Mix together with your fingertips to the consistency of fine breadcrumbs. Add the buttermilk and gently stir to combine until a dough forms. Add the raisins and knead lightly to spread them throughout the dough. Don't overwork the dough – the less you work it, the lighter the scones will be. Cover the bowl and set aside to rest for 10 minutes. This allows the dough to relax to avoid toughness.

Turn the dough out onto a lightly floured work surface and roll out to a thickness of 1 cm/⅜ inch. Stamp out rounds using the cookie cutter, turn them over and arrange on the prepared baking sheet. Bring any scraps of dough together, re-roll and stamp out as many rounds as you can.

Brush the tops of each round with a little beaten egg to glaze. Cover the baking sheets with a clean kitchen cloth and set aside in a warm place to rise and prove for 30 minutes.

Preheat the oven to 140°C fan/ 160°C/325°F/Gas 3.

Bake the scones in the preheated oven for about 30 minutes until a skewer inserted into the middle of a scone comes out clean. Transfer to a wire rack to cool.

Serve the scones warm or cold with jam/jelly and clotted cream. Best eaten on the day of baking.

Apple & cinnamon scones

Cinnamon is the perfect spice to pair with apples, bringing a subtle warmth to these scones. These scones are lovely served warm, spread with butter.

500 g/4 cups self-raising/rising flour, plus extra for dusting

100 g/6½ tablespoons butter, diced

a pinch of salt

50 g/¼ cup caster/granulated sugar

½ teaspoon ground cinnamon

1 Bramley apple, peeled, cored and diced

scant 300 ml/1¼ cups full-fat/whole milk

1 egg and 1 tablespoon milk, beaten together

a 4-cm/1½-inch round cookie cutter

a baking sheet, lined with parchment paper

MAKES 6-8

Preheat the oven to 180°C fan/200°C/400°F/Gas 6.

Sieve the flour into a large bowl and add the butter. Rub it lightly into the flour with your fingertips, lifting the mixture to aerate it as you work. When the mixture resembles fine breadcrumbs, add the salt, sugar and cinnamon and mix to combine. Stir in the apple.

Add just enough milk to bring the mixture together to form a soft (but not sticky) dough. Take care not to handle the dough too much or the scones will become heavy.

Lightly dust a work surface with flour and roll the dough out to about 3 cm/1 inch thick. Stamp out rounds with the cookie cutter. Try to avoid re-rolling the dough as this will make the scones heavy. Place the scones on the lined baking sheet and bake in the preheated oven for about 12-15 minutes, until risen and golden. Leave to cool a little on a wire rack. Best eaten on the day of baking.

Orange & cranberry scones

These American-style scones have so much butter and cream and fruit that it's impossible to cut them into perfect little shapes. The best way to deal with this super-rich and sticky dough is to cut it into triangular pie-slice shapes and then move the pieces gently around the baking sheet and bake. Serve with Seville orange marmalade – a perfect complement to the cranberries.

60 g/5 tablespoons caster/granulated sugar, plus extra for sprinkling

grated zest of 1 orange

530 g/3¾ cups plain/all-purpose flour

1½ teaspoons baking powder

½ teaspoon salt

350 g/3 sticks unsalted butter, cut into pea-sized cubes and chilled

3 eggs

1 egg yolk

185 ml/¾ cup whipping cream

100 g/¾ cup dried cranberries

a baking sheet, lined with parchment paper

MAKES ABOUT 12

Whiz the sugar and orange zest in an electric mixer with paddle attachment (or rub with your bare hands) until the sugar mells citrussy.

Add the flour, baking powder and salt and stir.

Add the cold butter to the flour mixture and rub between your fingertips (or in the mixer with paddle attachment) until you reach a sand-like consistency. Refrigerate for 20 minutes.

Preheat the oven to 150°C fan/170°C/340°F/Gas 3.

Put the whole eggs, egg yolk and cream in a separate bowl and beat lightly. Pour into the sandy flour mixture and add the cranberries. Fold until just combined. Be careful not to overmix at this stage, to ensure the scones stay nice and

soft. Keep in mind that the dough will be quite soft and sticky.

Sprinkle the baking sheet liberally with caster sugar.

Flip the dough out onto the lined baking sheet and sprinkle caster sugar on top. Pat down into a disc about 3 cm/1¼ inches high.

Using a sharp, serrated knife, cut the dough disc into fat wedges like a pie, and space them apart on the baking sheet. Bake in the preheated oven for 25–30 minutes until golden brown and solid when pressed.

Serve warm. Scones are best eaten on the day of baking.

Walnut & orange scones

Zesty orange, sweet spicy ginger and earthy walnuts combine
wonderfully in these scones. Mascarpone and fig preserve

225 g/1¾ cups self-raising/rising
   flour, plus extra for dusting

1 teaspoon baking powder

1½ tablespoons caster/granulated
   sugar

½ teaspoon ground ginger

75 g/5 tablespoons unsalted butter,
   chilled and diced

grated zest and freshly squeezed
   juice of 1 unwaxed orange

2 pieces of stem ginger, chopped

40 g/¼ cup walnut pieces

about 2 tablespoons milk, plus extra
   for brushing

1 egg

mascarpone and fig preserve,
   to serve

a 4-cm/1¾-inch round cookie cutter

a baking sheet, lined with
   parchment paper

MAKES 16

Preheat the oven to 200°C fan/
220°C/425°F/Gas 7.

Put the flour, baking powder, sugar
and ground ginger in a food
processor and pulse to combine.

Add the butter and process for
about 20 seconds until the mixture
resembles fine breadcrumbs.
Transfer to a large bowl and add
the zest, stem ginger and walnuts.
Combine well with a fork, then
make a well in the centre.

Pour the orange juice into a
measuring jug and add enough
milk to make it up to 100 ml/⅓ cup
plus 1 tablespoon. (Don't worry if
the mixture curdles slightly.) Beat
in the egg, then pour into the flour
mixture, bringing it together into
a soft dough using a fork.

Turn out onto a lightly floured
surface and knead briefly, working
in a little more flour to make a soft,
but not sticky dough. Gently pat or
roll out to 2.5 cm/1 inch thick and
cut out with the cookie cutter,
pressing the trimmings together to
make more scones. Arrange on the
baking sheet, spaced slightly apart.
Bake in the preheated oven for
about 10 minutes until risen and
golden. Transfer to a wire rack to
cool slightly. Serve warm with
mascarpone and fig preserve.

Peach melba scones

These dainty bite-sized scones are filled with peach preserve, fresh nectarines and raspberries and cream for a decadent teatime treat.

─── ◦ ◦ ◦ ───

100 g/¾ cup self-raising/rising flour

1 teaspoon baking powder

30 g/⅓ cup ground almond

30 g/2 tablespoons butter, chilled and cubed

2 teaspoons almond extract

30 g/2 generous tablespoons caster/ granulated sugar, plus extra for sprinkling

2–3 tablespoons full-fat/whole milk

TO SERVE

3–4 tablespoons clotted cream or whipped double/heavy cream

1 nectarine, thinly sliced

16 raspberries

3 tablespoons peach preserve

icing/confectioners' sugar, for dusting

a 5-cm/2-inch round cookie cutter

a large baking sheet, lined with parchment paper

MAKES 16

Preheat the oven to 160°C fan/ 180°C/350°F/Gas 4.

Sift the flour and baking powder into a bowl and add the ground almonds. Rub the butter into the mixture with your fingertips until it resembles fine breadcrumbs. Add half the almond extract, the sugar and 2 tablespoons milk and mix to form a soft dough. Add a little more milk if the mixture is too dry.

On a flour-dusted surface, roll out the dough to a thickness of 2 cm/¾ inch and cut out 16 rounds. Put the scones on the baking sheet a small distance apart. Use a pastry brush to glaze the tops of each round with the remaining milk mixed with the remaining almond extract. Sprinkle with sugar.

Bake in the preheated oven for 10–15 minutes until golden brown. Let cool on a wire rack, then cut in half and fill with clotted cream, nectarine slices, raspberries and a little peach preserve. Replace the tops and dust with sugar to serve.

Cheese & rosemary scones

These gluten-free scones are excellent served warm from the oven. Cheddar is recommended here, but any hard cheese can be grated or crumbled into the mix, and the herbs and spices varied to complement it. Why not try Stilton and chive, Manchego and basil or add 1 tablespoon of caster/granulated sugar instead of the mustard powder and give Wensleydale and dried cranberries a whirl? Perfect served with a large dollop of sticky and tangy red onion marmalade.

225 g/1½ cups plain/all-purpose gluten-free flour, plus extra for dusting

18 g/4½ teaspoons baking powder

½ teaspoon mustard powder

¼ teaspoon salt

¼ teaspoon xanthan gum

40 g/3 tablespoons unsalted butter, softened

60 g/2 oz. (about ¾ cup) grated/shredded Cheddar cheese

2 tablespoons fresh rosemary leaves, finely chopped

140 g/½ cup plus 1½ tablespoons buttermilk

1 egg

1 beaten egg, to glaze

butter and red onion marmalade, to serve (optional)

a 5–6-cm/2–2¼-inch round cookie cutter

a baking sheet, lined with parchment paper

MAKES 4–6

Preheat the oven to 170°C fan/ 190°C/375°F/Gas 5.

In a large bowl, or the bowl of a stand mixer, add the flour, baking powder, mustard powder, salt and xanthan gum. Add the butter in small pieces. Either rub in by hand or on a slow speed until the mixture resembles breadcrumbs and no large lumps of butter remain. Stir in the grated cheese and half of the rosemary.

In a jug/pitcher, combine the buttermilk and whole egg, then pour into the dry mixture. Stir together using a large metal spoon or on a slow speed. Once you have a sticky dough, stop mixing.

Dust the work surface well with extra flour and tip the dough onto it. Using your hands, briefly knead the dough and then gently press into a flat disc that's approximately 2–3 cm/1–1½ inches deep.

Stamp out scones from the dough using the cookie cutter. Push straight down and lift the cutter straight up, as twisting will prevent the scones from rising evenly in the oven.

Bring together the remaining dough and re-knead briefly, then stamp out more scones.

Transfer the scones to the lined baking sheet. Space them to allow for spreading and rising. Brush over the tops of the scones with the beaten egg to glaze, then sprinkle with the rest of the chopped rosemary.

Bake in the preheated oven for 15–20 minutes until risen, golden and firm to the touch. Gently lift a scone up from the sheet: the bottom should also be lightly browned and sound hollow when tapped. If required, return to the oven for 3–5 minutes more.

Allow to cool slightly on a wire rack before serving with lashings of butter and red onion marmalade. These scones are best eaten on the day they are made.

Triple cheese scones with whipped mustard butter

These savoury scones celebrate three different cheeses – Cheddar,
Gruyère and Parmesan – resulting in a really cheesy taste.
Served with a whipped mustard butter, they are just gorgeous
and very moreish. Some crispy pancetta sprinkled on top would
be very tasty, too.

---

350 g/2¾ cups plain/all-purpose
   flour

100 g/¾ cup spelt flour

3 teaspoons baking powder

½ rounded teaspoon English
   mustard powder

¼–½ teaspoon cayenne pepper

75 g/5 tablespoons butter, chilled
   and diced

50 g/½ cup coarsely grated/shredded
   Cheddar, plus extra for the
   topping

50 g/½ cup coarsely grated/shredded
   Gruyère

25 g/⅓ cup finely grated Parmesan,
   plus extra for the topping

125 ml/½ cup buttermilk

150 ml/⅔ cup full-fat/whole milk,
   plus 1 tablespoon for glazing

salt and freshly ground black pepper

MUSTARD BUTTER

125 g/1 stick butter, softened

1 teaspoon English mustard

1 teaspoon grainy mustard

2 teaspoons finely snipped fresh
   chives

a 5-cm/2-inch round cookie cutter

a baking sheet, lined with
   parchment paper

MAKES ABOUT 18

First make the mustard butter. Beat the butter in a bowl with a wooden spoon until really light and creamy. Add both types of mustard and season with salt and black pepper. Mix to combine, then add the chopped chives. Lay a sheet of clingfilm/plastic wrap or parchment paper on the work surface and lay the butter on top in a rough sausage shape. Roll the butter into a neat log roughly 2 cm/$\frac{3}{4}$ inch in diameter. Twist the ends to seal and chill the butter for about 2 hours until firm.

Preheat the oven to 180°C fan/ 200°C/400°F/Gas 6.

Sift both flours, baking powder, mustard powder and cayenne pepper into a large mixing bowl. Season well with black pepper and a pinch of salt. Add the chilled, diced butter and rub into the dry ingredients using your fingertips. When there are only very small specks of butter still visible, add the grated/shredded cheeses and mix to combine.

Make a well in the middle of the mixture and pour in the buttermilk and milk. Use a palette knife to mix into a dough, then very lightly bring the mixture together with your hands to a rough ball.

Turn the dough out onto a lightly floured surface and knead for 10 seconds. Flatten or roll out to a thickness of 1.5–2 cm/$\frac{5}{8}$–$\frac{3}{4}$ inch. Use the cookie cutter to stamp out rounds and arrange on the prepared baking sheet, leaving a little space inbetween to allow for spreading during baking. Gather the dough scraps into a ball, re-roll and stamp out more scones. Brush the top of the scones with a little milk, scatter with the extra cheeses and a pinch of cayenne pepper.

Bake on the middle shelf of the preheated oven for about 13–15 minutes until well-risen and golden brown. Cool on a wire rack.

Split the scones in half and spread with the mustard butter to serve.

Chapter 3
Small Cakes
& Cookies

Fraises-des-bois friands

*These moist and very moreish friands are made extra special
by the addition of tiny woodland or wild strawberries that
appear in early summer – a marriage made in heaven. You'll
need to use special baking moulds for these delights.*

$\rightarrow$ · · · $\leftarrow$

70 g/½ cup ground almonds
30 g/¼ cup plain/all-purpose flour
a pinch of salt
120 g/1 cup icing/confectioners'
   sugar
100 g/6½ tablespoons butter
3 egg whites
80 g/3 oz. fraises des bois
   (wild strawberries)

6 friand moulds, lightly greased

MAKES 6

Preheat the oven to 160°C fan/
180°C/350°F/Gas 4.

Mix the almonds, flour, salt and
sugar in a large bowl.

Melt the butter in a small saucepan,
then remove from the heat and
leave to cool. Whisk the egg whites
until frothy and light (it's not
necessary to whip them into peaks
as you would if making meringues).

Trickle the butter into the dry
ingredients and add half the egg
whites. Mix lightly, and then add
the remaining egg whites and
continue to mix until they are
fully incorporated.

Spoon the mixture into the
prepared moulds and scatter the
fraises des bois over the top. Bake
in the preheated oven for about
15 minutes or so, until the friands
are risen and golden and spring
back when pressed lightly.

Serve warm or leave to cool
completely.

Almond financiers

Financiers are delightful little cakes that are very similar to friands (see page 70), but financiers are generally made with beurre noisette (butter that is heated to a lovely amber colour with an appealing nutty aroma).

70 g/½ cup ground almonds
30 g/¼ cup plain/all-purpose flour
a pinch of salt
120 g/1 generous cup icing/
   confectioners' sugar
grated zest of 2 lemons
100 g/6½ tablespoons butter
3 egg whites
50 g/½ cup flaked/slivered almonds

6 mini loaf pans or small muffin
   moulds, lightly greased

MAKES 6

Preheat the oven to 160°C fan/
180°C/350°F/Gas 4.

Mix the ground almonds/almond meal, flour, salt and sugar in a large bowl. Stir in the lemon zest.

Melt the butter in a small saucepan and leave it over the heat until it turns to an amber colour and gives off a nutty aroma. Remove it from the heat and leave to cool slightly. Whisk the egg whites until frothy and light (no need to whip to stiff peaks as when making meringues).

Trickle the butter into the dry ingredients and add half the egg whites. Mix lightly, and then add the remaining egg whites and continue to mix until fully incorporated.

Spoon the mixture into the prepared pans and scatter the flaked/slivered almonds over the top. Bake for about 15 minutes, until they are risen and golden and spring back when pressed lightly. Serve warm, or leave to cool completely.

Mini madeleines with citrus posset

Posset has its origins in Medieval England and this syllabub-like dessert is still popular today. Serve in small glasses with a side order of dainty orange madeleines.

POSSET

600 ml/2½ cups double/heavy cream

200 g/1 cup caster/granulated sugar

finely grated zest and juice of 2 small oranges and 2 lemons

2 teaspoons finely chopped fresh mint

MADELEINES

2 eggs

80 g/⅓ cup caster/granulated sugar

100 g/¾ cup plus 1 tablespoon self-raising/rising flour

1 tablespoon honey

zest of 1 orange

1 teaspoon vanilla extract

100 g/7 tablespoons butter, melted and cooled

12 small shot glasses

a piping/pastry bag

2 x 20-hole/cup mini madeleine pans, well greased

SERVES 12

To make the posset, put the cream, sugar, orange and lemon zests and mint in a saucepan and heat for about 3–5 minutes, until the sugar has dissolved. Bring to the boil and then strain into a large jug/pitcher through a fine mesh sieve/strainer to remove the mint and zest. Whisk in the orange and lemon juices, then pour into the glasses. Chill in the fridge for 3–4 hours, until the posset is set.

To make the madeleines, whisk together the eggs and sugar until light and creamy. Sift in the flour, add the honey, orange zest and vanilla extract and whisk again. Pour in the cooled melted butter and fold in using a spatula. Spoon the mixture into the piping/pastry bag. Chill in the fridge for 1 hour.

Preheat the oven to 160°C fan/ 180°C/350°F/Gas 4. Pipe a little of the mixture into each hole in the madeleine pan and bake in the

preheated oven for 10–15 minutes, until golden brown. (If you only have one madeleine pan, bake in batches, storing the uncooked batter in the fridge whilst the first batch is cooking.) Turn the madeleines out onto a wire rack and leave to cool.

Serve a glass of chilled posset with 3 madeleines on the side for each serving (you will have a few extra madeleines leftover for second helpings). The madeleines and posset are both best eaten fresh, on the day they are made.

Raspberry & clotted cream whirls

A special afternoon tea deserves an indulgent sweet treat and these buttery crisp whirls – sometimes known as Viennese whirls – deliciously filled with thick clotted cream and juicy fresh raspberries fit the bill wonderfully.

250 g/2 sticks soft butter

200 g/1⅔ cups plain/all-purpose flour

50 g/½ cup cornflour/cornstarch

50 g/scant ½ cup icing/confectioners' sugar

1 teaspoon vanilla extract

FILLING

300 g/1¼ cups clotted cream

250 g/2 cups raspberries

caster/granulated sugar, for dusting

2 baking sheets, lined with baking parchment

a piping/pastry bag fitted with a star nozzle/tip

MAKES ABOUT 10

Preheat the oven to 160°C fan/180°C/350°F/Gas 4.

Mix the butter, flours, icing/confectioners' sugar and vanilla extract together until it forms a smooth dough. Spoon the mixture into a piping/pastry bag and pipe round shapes, about 5 cm/2 inches in diameter, onto the prepared baking sheets.

Bake in the preheated oven for about 15 minutes, until golden. Remove from the oven and leave to cool for a few minutes, then transfer to a wire rack until completely cold.

To serve, sandwich together with clotted cream and raspberries and dust lightly with sugar.

Black Forest fondant fancies

Fondant fancies are an absolute must for afternoon tea, and this recipe is a world away from the shop-bought versions. These have a 'Black Forest' twist with the addition of chocolate, cherries and Kirsch.

150 g/1 stick plus 2 tablespoons butter, softened

100 g/½ cup caster/granulated sugar

100 g/½ cup soft light brown sugar

3 eggs, lightly beaten

1 teaspoon vanilla extract

200 g/1⅔ cups plain/all-purpose flour

½ teaspoon bicarbonate of soda/baking soda

1 teaspoon baking powder

a pinch of salt

40 g/⅓ cup cocoa powder

3–4 tablespoons boiling water

3 tablespoons full-fat/whole milk

5 tablespoons cherry jam/jelly

100 g/3½ oz. marzipan

50 g/1½ oz. white chocolate, melted, to decorate

VANILLA & KIRSCH BUTTERCREAM

125 g/1 stick butter, softened

150 g/1 cup icing/confectioners' sugar

1 tablespoon Kirsch

1 teaspoon vanilla bean paste

CHOCOLATE FONDANT

500 g/3½ cups fondant icing/confectioners' sugar

3 tablespoons cocoa powder

a 20-cm/8-inch square cake pan, greased and lined with buttered baking parchment

1–2 disposable piping/pastry bags

MAKES 16

Preheat the oven to 160°C fan/ 180°C/350°F/Gas 4.

Cream the butter with both sugars in a stand mixer for 3–4 minutes until pale and light. Scrape down the bowl with a rubber spatula and gradually add the beaten eggs, mixing well between each addition. Add the vanilla extract and mix again until combined.

Sift in the flour, bicarbonate of soda/baking soda and baking powder, and add the salt. Mix the cocoa powder with the boiling water, then add to the mixture with the milk, and beat until smooth. Spoon the mixture into the prepared cake pan and spread level with the back of a spoon.

Bake on the middle shelf of the preheated oven for 30–35 minutes or until a skewer inserted into the middle of the cake comes out clean. Cool in the pan, then turn out of the pan, peel off the baking parchment, turn the cake the right way up and leave to cool completely on a wire rack.

To prepare the vanilla and Kirsch buttercream, beat the butter until very soft, pale and light. Gradually add the icing/confectioners' sugar, mixing well between each addition. When it has all been incorporated add the Kirsch and the vanilla bean paste. Mix again.

Using a serrated knife, slice the rounded top off the cake to give it a totally flat and smooth top, then cut the cake in half horizontally. Carefully lift the top half of the cake off and set aside.

Using a palette knife, spread half of the buttercream in a smooth layer on the bottom cake layer. Top the buttercream with half of the cherry jam/jelly and replace the top cake layer. Gently press together, then spread the remaining cherry jam/jelly on top.

Lightly dust the work surface with icing/confectioners' sugar and roll out the marzipan to a 20-cm/ 8-inch square. Carefully lift over the cake covering the jam/jelly.

Using the serrated knife, trim the edges of the cake, then cut into 16 squares.

Spoon the remaining buttercream into one of the piping/pastry bags and pipe a small mound of buttercream on top of each square.

To make the chocolate fondant, sift the fondant icing/confectioners' sugar and cocoa powder into a mixing bowl, and whisking constantly, add enough water to make an icing that coats the back of a spoon.

Taking one square cake at a time, spear it onto a large fork and spoon the fondant over the top and sides of the cake, allowing any excess to drip back into the bowl. Gently tap the fork on the side of the bowl to allow any excess icing to run down the sides, then carefully slide the cake off the fork onto a wire rack set over a sheet of baking parchment. Repeat with the remaining cakes, then leave them to dry for 1 hour.

Drizzle the melted white chocolate over the cakes and leave to set before serving.

Clotted cream & raspberry brûlée tartlets

Make these delicate brûlée tarts with the freshest, largest, juiciest rapsberries you can find.

⊹ • • • ⊹

SHORTCRUST PASTRY

150 g/1 cup plus 2 tablespoons plain/all-purpose flour, plus extra for dusting

150 g/1 stick plus 2 tablespoons butter

75 g/$\frac{1}{3}$ cup caster/superfine sugar

75 g/$\frac{1}{2}$ cup plus 1 tablespoon rice flour

grated zest of $\frac{1}{2}$ lemon

FILLING

1 vanilla pod/bean

2 egg yolks

200 g/scant 1 cup clotted cream

80 g/$\frac{1}{3}$ cup caster/superfine sugar

a pinch of flaky sea salt

250 g/2 cups fresh raspberries

3 tablespoons icing/ confectioners' sugar

6 tartlet pans with removable base, about 6.5-cm/2$\frac{1}{2}$-inch diameter

a cook's blow torch

MAKES 6

To make the pastry, in a bowl rub together the flour, butter, sugar and rice flour until the mixture looks like breadcrumbs. Stir in the lemon zest and bring it together to form a dough. Wrap in clingfilm/plastic wrap and chill in the fridge until firm. When firm, roll out on a lightly floured surface and line the tartlet pans, then return them to the fridge to chill.

Preheat the oven to 160°C fan/ 180°C/350°F/Gas 4.

For the filling, split the vanilla pod/bean lengthways and scrape out the seeds. Beat the egg yolks, clotted cream, sugar, vanilla seeds and salt until smooth.

Bake the pastry bases in the preheated oven for 6–8 minutes, until firm and pale golden. If the pastry has risen up slightly, push it back carefully against the edges with a teaspoon. Remove from the oven and scatter the raspberries over the bases. Pour in the custard filling. Bake for 10–15 minutes until the custard is just set. Remove from the oven and cool.

Sprinkle a fine layer of icing/confectioners' sugar over the top of each tart and caramelize carefully with a blow torch, taking care not to burn any raspberries that may be peeping out of the custard. Serve within a couple of hours, so that the brûlée top remains crisp.

Vegan brownies

These dark, dense brownies are sure to delight chocolate-loving vegans, but they will also surprise conventional brownie fans, too. They are fab served with a cuppa and a few fresh raspberries.

200 g/7 oz. dark/bittersweet chocolate, melted

250 ml/1 cup plus 1 tablespoon just-boiled water

100 ml/⅓ cup plus 1 tablespoon sunflower oil

375 g/2 cups minus 2 tablespoons light brown muscovado sugar

1 teaspoon cider vinegar

2 teaspoons vanilla bean paste

175 g/1⅓ cups plain/all-purpose flour

½ teaspoon baking powder

a 30 x 17 x 2.5-cm/11¾ x 6¾ x 1-inch brownie pan, lightly greased and lined with parchment paper

MAKES 15

Preheat the oven to 150°C fan/170°C/325°F/Gas 3.

Pour the melted chocolate into a large bowl and slowly whisk in the just-boiled water. Whisk in the sunflower oil. Beat in the muscovado sugar, and then add the cider vinegar and vanilla bean paste. Stir in the flour and baking powder.

Pour the mixture into the prepared pan and bake in the preheated oven for about 45 minutes, until the top of the brownie feels squidgy but set. Leave to cool in the pan, before cutting into squares. Store in an airtight container, making sure to separate any layers with parchment paper if necessary.

Raspberry brownies

There's an art to making the perfect gooey, crunchy brownie. The gooeyness is all about timing; using a thermometer takes the guesswork out of this. The key to the crunchy top is whisking your eggs until they are foaming and hold their bubbles and, most importantly, using the freshest eggs you can find. These brownies also work well using a good-quality gluten-free flour.

300 g/2¾ sticks butter

300 g/10½ oz. good-quality dark/
   bittersweet chocolate

5 eggs

400 g/2 cups caster/granulated
   sugar

30 g/⅓ cup unsweetened cocoa
   powder

150 g/1 generous cup plain/
   all-purpose flour or
   gluten-free flour

RASPBERRIES

200 g/1⅓ cups raspberries

50 g/¼ cup caster/granulated sugar

freshly squeezed juice of ½ lemon

a non-stick 30 x 20-cm/12 x 8-inch
   brownie pan, lightly oiled and
   lined with parchment paper

MAKES 10

Place the raspberries in a bowl with the sugar and lemon juice in advance. Stir, then leave to infuse for 30 minutes or longer.

Preheat the oven to 120°C fan/ 140°C/280°F/Gas 1.

Place the butter in a saucepan and melt over a low heat. Once the butter is fully melted, break the chocolate up into individual pieces and add to the melted butter. Leave for a few minutes, then stir together to form a thick chocolate ganache sauce. Leave the sauce to cool for 20 minutes.

Place the eggs and sugar in a large mixing bowl and whisk using a hand-held electric whisk until thick, smooth and creamy.

Add the chocolate sauce and the cocoa, and whisk to combine the ingredients until the mixture is

thick and even. With a wooden spoon, fold in the flour until the mixture is smooth.

Place the soaked raspberries in the brownie pan and carefully cover them with the brownie mixture (if they poke through the top they will catch and burn).

Bake in the preheated oven for 20–25 minutes. The brownies are cooked when the mixture has a core temperature of 90°C/195°F; they should still have a little bit of a wobble. Cool for 30 minutes at room temperature. To slice without cracking the top too much, chill in the fridge for a few hours before cutting into squares to serve.

To enjoy them warm, reheat for 15 seconds in a microwave and serve with cream or ice cream.

Bijoux blondies

Using extra virgin olive oil in the brownie mixture renders a rich, deliciously tender texture. Use the finest quality white chocolate you can find with as little sugar as possible for the best result. This recipe is best made the day before as the cooked brownies need to chill in the fridge overnight.

---

250 g/9 oz. white chocolate, chopped

120 g/1 stick butter, chopped

½ tablespoon mild extra virgin olive oil

4 eggs

140 g/¾ cup caster/granulated sugar

90 g/⅔ cup plain/all-purpose flour

70 g/½ cup blanched almonds, chopped

blanched almonds, to decorate

WHITE CHOCOLATE & OLIVE OIL GANACHE

1 vanilla pod/bean

90 ml/⅓ cup single/light cream

180 g/6½ oz. white chocolate, chopped

40 ml/3 tablespoons mild extra virgin olive oil

a 20-cm/8-inch square baking pan, greased and dusted with flour

MAKES 6–8

Preheat the oven to 150°C fan/170°C/325°F/Gas 3.

Put the white chocolate and butter in a heatproof bowl set over a saucepan of barely simmering water. Do not let the base of the bowl touch the water. Allow to melt, stirring occasionally, until completely smooth. Stir in the olive oil. Remove from the heat.

In a separate bowl, whisk the eggs and sugar for 1–2 minutes. Sift in the flour and whisk again to mix. Pour the chocolate mixture in and mix well with a wooden spoon. Finally, stir in the chopped almonds.

Spoon the mixture into the prepared baking pan, spread level with a spatula and bake in the preheated oven for about 20 minutes. Allow to cool completely in the pan.

To make the white chocolate and olive oil ganache, split the vanilla pod/bean lengthways and scrape the

seeds out into a saucepan. Add the cream and gently bring to the boil. Meanwhile, put the chocolate in a heatproof bowl set over a saucepan of barely simmering water. Do not let the base of the bowl touch the water. Allow to melt, stirring occasionally, until completely smooth. Add the olive oil and stir in. Remove from the heat and pour in the boiled cream. Beat with an

electric whisk until smooth and glossy. Spread the ganache evenly over the cold brownie in the pan and refrigerate overnight.

When you are ready to serve, cut the brownie into equal portions and decorate each one with a blanched almond.

Rocky road slices

All the comfortingly indulgent flavours of rocky road ice cream – chocolate, nuts and marshmallows – are encapsulated here.

60 g/⅓ cup caster/granulated sugar

60 g/½ stick butter, softened

1 egg

60 g/½ cup self-raising/rising flour

1 tablespoon buttermilk

30 g/1 oz. dark/bittersweet chocolate, grated

150 ml/⅔ cup double/heavy cream, whipped

CHOCOLATE GLAZE

30 g/2 tablespoons butter

60 ml/¼ cup golden/light corn syrup

70 g/2½ oz. dark/bittersweet chocolate, broken into pieces

TO DECORATE

mini marshmallows

glacé cherries, halved

white chocolate chips

chopped walnuts

a 20-cup/hole silicone mini loaf tray/pan, greased

a piping/pastry bag, fitted with a large star nozzle/tip

MAKES 10

Preheat the oven to 160°C fan/180°C/350°F/Gas 4.

Whisk together the sugar and butter until light and creamy. Whisk in the egg. Sift in the flour and fold in, along with the buttermilk and grated chocolate. Spoon the mixture into the loaf pan and bake in the preheated oven for 10–12 minutes, until the cakes spring back to the touch. Let cool in the pan.

To prepare the chocolate glaze, heat the butter, syrup and chocolate in a saucepan until the chocolate has melted. To assemble, spoon the whipped cream into the piping/pastry bag. Turn out the cooled cakes from the pan and pipe small stars of cream onto half of the cakes. Top with the remaining cakes and cover with the chocolate glaze.

Decorate the cakes with the mini marshmallows, cherries, white chocolate chips and walnuts. Pile as high as you can for the best effect. Serve immediately or store in the fridge until needed.

Shortbread

Crisp and buttery, these simple-to-make biscuits have long been a favourite. This recipe uses cornflour/cornstarch for a creamier texture and rice flour to give a crisper bite. There is nothing better to enjoy with a cup of tea, or to serve with whipped cream and fresh strawberries for a summer tea.

165 g/1½ sticks salted butter, firm but not hard

85 g/scant ½ cup caster/granulated sugar

200 g/1½ cups plus 2 tablespoons plain/all-purpose flour, plus extra for dusting

5 teaspoons cornflour/cornstarch

35 g/¼ cup rice flour

a pinch of salt

whipped cream and sliced strawberries, to serve

a 5-cm/2-inch round cookie cutter

a baking sheet, lined with parchment paper

MAKES 20

Preheat the oven to 150°C fan/170°C/325°F/Gas 3.

In a large bowl, cream the butter and sugar together until pale and fluffy. Sift the flour, cornflour/cornstarch and rice flour into another bowl, then add a quarter of the total flours to the creamed butter and stir in. Add another quarter of the flour and begin rubbing the mixture together using your fingertips. Add the remaining flour and mix again with your fingers. Knead gently into a malleable ball of dough. This can also be done by putting all the ingredients in a food processor and blending until it forms a smooth ball of dough.

Tip the dough out onto a lightly floured surface and roll it out until about 1 cm/½ inch thick (roll a little thinner if you will be sandwiching the shortbreads together with cream). Stamp out

discs with the cookie cutter and arrange about 4 cm/1½ inches apart on the prepared baking sheet. Re-roll any leftover dough and cut out discs, as before, until all the dough is used up. Bake in the preheated oven for 20 minutes or until the base of the shortbread is golden and the top almost firm to the touch. Remove from the oven and allow to cool and set on the baking sheet before eating or storing.

To serve, sandwich the shortbreads together with a filling of whipped cream and sliced strawberries.

The plain shortbread will keep for 7–10 days in an airtight container or freeze for up to 2 months.

Butterfly cakes

Ring the changes with these classic cakes by making a selection of flavours; shown below is the recipe for orange, with vanilla and chocolate variations, but you could try coffee or lemon too.

ORANGE BUTTERFLY CAKES

100 g/6½ tablespoons salted butter, softened

100 g/½ cup caster/granulated sugar

grated zest of 1 orange

2 eggs

100 g/¾ cup self-raising/rising flour

ORANGE FILLING

100 g/6½ tablespoons salted butter, softened

200 g/1⅓ cups icing/confectioners' sugar

grated zest of 1 orange, plus the juice of ½ orange

a 12-hole cake pan, lined with paper cases

a piping/pastry bag (optional)

MAKES 12

Preheat the oven to 170°C fan/ 190°C/375°F/Gas 5.

Using an electric hand whisk, cream the butter, sugar and orange zest together in a large mixing bowl until pale and fluffy. Add the eggs one at a time, beating well between each addition. With the whisk on slow speed, gradually add the flour and mix to a smooth, creamy consistency.

Spoon the mixture into the paper cases and bake in the preheated oven for 12–15 minutes or until golden brown and the tops spring back from light finger pressure. Remove from the oven and transfer to a wire rack to cool.

To make the filling, beat the butter, icing/confectioners' sugar, orange juice and zest together with an electric hand whisk. Start on slow speed and increase to high speed when all the sugar is incorporated, beating for about 2–3 minutes in total.

When the cakes have cooled, slice the top off them, then cut each top in half to form wings. Pipe or spoon the buttercream onto the top of the cakes and place the wings on top. Dust icing/confectioners' sugar over them. The cakes are best eaten on the day of baking.

Vanilla variation

Add $\frac{1}{4}$ teaspoon vanilla extract in place of the orange zest. For the vanilla filling, mix 1 teaspoon vanilla extract and 2 tablespoons water together and add to the butter and sugar in place of the orange juice and zest.

Chocolate variation

Stir 1 tablespoon each cocoa powder and water together to form a paste and add to the butter and sugar in place of the orange zest. For the chocolate filling, mix 2 tablespoons cocoa powder and 1 tablespoon water together to form a paste and add to the butter and sugar in place of orange juice and zest.

Pavlova cupcakes

The beloved pavlova dessert was invented to honour the Russian ballerina, Anna Pavlova, and this vanilla cupcake rendition is an ode to her elegance and grace. Start this recipe the day before, as it needs overnight chilling in the fridge.

½ vanilla pod/bean

3 eggs

150 g/1 cup icing/confectioners' sugar

150 g/1 cup plus 2 tablespoons plain/all-purpose flour

1 teaspoon baking powder

150 g/1 stick plus 3 tablespoons butter, melted

fresh raspberries, meringue chips, finely chopped freeze-dried raspberries and edible silver lustre dust, to decorate

VANILLA CHANTILLY

1 vanilla pod/bean

450 ml/1¾ cups whipping cream

45 g/5 tablespoons icing/confectioners' sugar

a 12-hole cupcake pan, lined with paper cases

a piping/pastry bag, fitted with a star-shaped nozzle/tip

MAKES 12

To make the vanilla cupcake mixture, start the day before you want to bake the cupcakes. Split the vanilla pod/bean lengthways and scrape the seeds out into a bowl. Add the eggs and sugar and beat with an electric whisk until it has tripled in volume and the beaters leave a thick ribbon trail when you lift them out of the mixture.

Sift the flour and baking powder into the bowl and whisk lightly. Add the melted butter and fold in gently with a large metal spoon. Cover and refrigerate for 24 hours.

The next day, preheat the oven to 140°C fan/160°C/325°F/Gas 3.

Divide the mixture between the cupcake cases and bake in the preheated oven for about 15–20 minutes. Remove from the oven and allow to cool completely.

To make the vanilla chantilly, split the vanilla pod/bean lengthways and scrape the seeds out into a bowl. Add the cream and sugar and beat with an electric whisk until it is firm enough to pipe.

Fill the piping/pastry bag with the chantilly and pipe on top of the cooled cupcakes. Decorate with fresh raspberries, meringue chips and freeze-dried raspberries and dust with edible silver lustre dust.

Cherry bakewell cupcakes

Introducing the cherry bakewell cupcake – moist, almondy and enticing, this has all the classic flavours of a cherry backewell slice in cupcake form. What's not to love? We've included a recipe for making your own marzipan, but if you prefer, you can use a good-quality shop-bought one.

240 ml/1 cup full-fat/whole milk

15 g/1 tablespoon sunflower oil

2 eggs

$\frac{1}{2}$ teaspoon almond extract

130 g/$3\frac{1}{2}$ oz. marzipan, grated (see right if making your own)

260 g/$1\frac{3}{4}$ cups plain/all-purpose gluten-free flour

14 g/$3\frac{1}{2}$ teaspoons baking powder

$\frac{1}{4}$ teaspoon salt

$\frac{3}{8}$ teaspoon xanthan gum

250 g/$1\frac{1}{4}$ cups caster/granulated sugar

70 g/5 tablespoons unsalted butter, softened

150 g/$\frac{2}{3}$ cup cherry jam/jelly, to fill

250 g/$2\frac{1}{4}$ cups royal icing/ confectioners' sugar

12 glacé cherries, to decorate

MARZIPAN

100 g/$\frac{1}{2}$ cup caster/granulated sugar

100 g/1 scant cup icing/ confectioners' sugar

150 g/1 cup ground almonds

1 egg

1–2 teaspoons almond extract, to taste

a 12-hole muffin pan, lined with paper cases

MAKES 12

If making your own marzipan, do so at least an hour in advance of baking the cupcakes. In a large bowl, or the bowl of a stand mixer, add the sugars and ground almonds. Add the egg and a quarter or half of the almond extract. Beat until everything comes together as a dough, adding a little extra icing/confectioners' sugar and ground almonds – a tablespoon at time of each, if the mixture seems too wet. Wrap in clingfilm/plastic wrap and chill in the fridge for at least 1 hour.

Preheat the oven to 170°C fan/ 190°C/375°F/Gas 5.

In a jug/pitcher, combine the milk, oil, eggs and almond extract.

Weigh out the marzipan and grate coarsely. The remainder can be stored in the fridge wrapped in clingfilm/plastic wrap.

In a large bowl, or the bowl of a stand mixer, add the flour, baking powder, salt, xanthan gum, sugar and softened butter. Using an electric handwhisk or the stand mixer, slowly mix the dry ingredients and the butter until they resemble fine breadcrumbs. Continue to mix on a slow speed and pour in the wet ingredients. Increase the speed and mix for 3–5 minutes until the batter thickens. Add the grated marzipan

and mix until evenly distributed through the batter. Divide the mixture between the cases; you want them to be around two-thirds full. (If there's a little batter remaining, use to make a couple of extra cupcakes).

Bake in the preheated oven for 12–15 minutes or until golden brown and the tops spring back with light finger pressure. Remove from the oven and transfer to a wire rack to cool.

Once cooled, carefully make a hollow in each cake, fill the hollows with a spoonful of cherry jam/jelly, then replace the sponge lid back on top.

Now make the royal icing. With an electric hand whisk or stand mixer, slowly mix together the royal icing sugar with 2 tablespoons of water. Whisk for 5–8 minutes until it stands in shiny, stiff peaks.

Use a spoon or palette knife to apply a smooth layer of royal icing to the cupcakes. Add a glacé cherry on top of each and allow to set before serving.

Lemon-basil cupcakes

This is the perfect cupcake to make when wild strawberries are in season. This vanilla-lemon cupcake is topped with a very light and summery lemon basil cream, which complements the tiny strawberries to perfection.

1 quantity Vanilla Cupcake Mixture (see pages 92–93, but follow the method here)

grated zest of $\frac{1}{2}$ lemon

wild strawberries and freshly chopped basil, to decorate

LEMON BASIL CREAM

220 g/$\frac{3}{4}$ cup lemon jam/jelly (yes jam, not curd!)

5 fresh basil leaves

250 g/9 oz. mascarpone

a 12-hole cupcake pan, lined with paper cases

a piping/pastry bag, fitted with a star-shaped nozzle/tip

MAKES 12

To make the vanilla cupcake mixture, start the day before you baking. Make the mixture as described on page 93 and fold in the lemon zest at the end. Cover and refrigerate for 24 hours.

The next day, preheat the oven to 140°C fan/160°C/325°F/Gas 3.

Divide the mixture between the cupcake cases and bake in the preheated oven for about 15–20 minutes. Remove from the oven and allow to cool completely.

To make the lemon basil cream, put the lemon jam and basil leaves in a food processor and blitz until smooth. Fold this gently into the mascarpone until evenly mixed. Fill the piping/pastry bag with the lemon basil cream and pipe on top of the cold cupcakes. Decorate with wild strawberries and chopped basil.

Vanilla butter cookies

These little buttery, vanilla-speckled cookies go very well with any kind of chamomile tea, renowned for its calming and digestive properties. So easy to make, these cookies can be baked a few days in advance as they store well in an airtight container.

2 vanilla pods/beans

200 g/1¾ sticks butter, softened

100 g/½ cup caster/granulated sugar, plus extra for dusting

300 g/2¼ cups plain/all-purpose flour

2–3 cookie sheets, lined with parchment paper

MAKES 20–25

Preheat the oven to 160°C fan/180°C/350°F/Gas 4.

Split the vanilla pods/beans lengthways and scrape out the seeds. Cream the butter, vanilla seeds and sugar until smooth, then stir in the flour until fully combined.

Break off pieces of dough about the size of a walnut and roll each one into a ball. Place on the prepared cookie sheets, leaving a little gap between each to allow for slight spreading. Push the tines of a fork into the dough to flatten it slightly and bake in the preheated oven for about 10–13 minutes, until golden and firm. If you wish, dust with caster/granulated sugar.

Transfer to a wire rack to cool. Store in an airtight container until ready to serve.

Lemon cookies

These lovely lemon treats are quick and easy to make. They are also great for home freezing, so it's worth baking an extra batch if you have the space.

150 g/1¼ sticks salted butter, firm but not hard

90 g/scant ½ cup golden caster/granulated sugar

170 g/1⅓ cups self-raising/rising flour

55 g/scant ½ cup plain/all-purpose flour, plus extra for dusting

finely grated zest of 2 lemons

5-cm/2-inch round cookie cutter

a baking sheet, lined with parchment paper

MAKES 18–20

Preheat the oven to 150°C fan/170°C/325°F/Gas 3.

In a large bowl, cream the butter and sugar together until pale and fluffy. Sift the flours into another bowl. Add a quarter of the total flour to the creamed butter and stir in. Add another quarter of the flour and the lemon zest and begin rubbing the mixture together using your fingertips. Add the remaining flour, and mix again with your fingers. Knead gently into a malleable ball of dough. This can also be done by putting all the ingredients in a food processor and blending until it forms a smooth ball of dough.

Put the dough on a lightly floured surface and roll it out until about 1 cm/½ inch thick. Stamp out discs with the cookie cutter and arrange them 4 cm/1½ inches apart on the prepared baking sheet. Re-roll any leftover dough and cut out cookies, as before, until all the dough is used up.

Bake in the preheated oven for 20 minutes, or until the bases of the cookies are golden and the tops are almost firm to the touch. Remove from the oven and allow to cool and set on the baking sheet before eating or storing.

The cookies will keep for 7–10 days in an airtight container or freeze for up to 2 months.

Rose thins

Rose extract adds a beautiful floral note to these cookies – it is fragrant, sweet and delicate. The cookie thins look so pretty decorated with rose petals.

100 g/7 tablespoons butter, softened

75 g/6 tablespoons caster/ granulated sugar

1 egg

150 g/generous 1 cup plain/ all-purpose flour, plus extra for dusting

1 teaspoon rose extract

candied rose petals, to decorate

icing/confectioners' sugar, for dusting

a 5-cm/2-inch cookie cutter

2 baking sheets, lined with parchment paper

MAKES 20

Preheat the oven to 140°C fan/ 160°C/325°F/Gas 3.

Whisk all of the ingredients together in a mixing bowl to form a smooth mixture. Roll into a ball, wrap in clingfilm/plastic wrap and chill in the fridge for an hour.

On a lightly floured surface, roll the mixture out to a thickness of about 3 mm/$\frac{1}{8}$ inch. Using the cookie cutter, cut out rounds and place on the lined baking sheets. Re-roll any leftover dough and cut out cookies, as before, until all the dough is used up.

Bake in the preheated oven for 10–12 minutes, until the thins are just starting to turn golden.

Serve decorated with the candied rose petals and dusted with sugar.

Chapter 4
Pastries
& Dainties

Blackcurrant millefeuilles

In a twist on the traditional millefeuille filling of vanilla custard, these pastries contain blackcurrant preserve – a sharp fruity burst perfectly offsetting the cream and sugar dusting.

❧ • • • ❧

flour, for dusting

375-g/13-oz. package all-butter puff pastry/dough, thawed if frozen

1 egg, beaten

caster/superfine sugar, for sprinkling

FILLING

200 ml/¾ cup double/heavy cream

2 generous tablespoons blackcurrant preserve

icing/confectioners' sugar, for dusting

a baking sheet, greased and lined with parchment paper

a piping/pastry bag, fitted with a star nozzle/tip

MAKES 24

Preheat the oven to 160°C fan/ 180°C/350°F/Gas 4.

On a flour-dusted surface, roll out the pastry to a thickness of 3 mm/ ⅛ in. Cut into six strips of 30 x 4 cm/ 12 x 2 in and transfer to the baking sheet using a large spatula, leaving a gap between each strip. Brush with the beaten egg and sprinkle over a little caster/superfine sugar.

Bake in the preheated oven for 12–15 minutes, until the pastry has risen and is golden brown on top. Transfer to a wire rack and let cool completely.

To serve, cut each pastry strip into 8 small squares. Whip the cream to stiff peaks, then spoon into the piping/pastry bag. Pipe a row of small cream stars onto half of the squares, top with a small spoonful of blackcurrant preserve, then cover with a second pastry square. Repeat until all the pastry squares are filled. Dust the tops with icing/ confectioners' sugar. Serve immediately or store in the fridge.

Mango & coconut millefeuilles

Mango really benefits from a dressing of fresh lime juice and here it is paired with a crème diplomat made with coconut milk for a tropical feel. With a brûléed top, the puff pastry layers have been baked between two baking sheets with icing/ confectioners' sugar to caramelize to give you a level millefeuille.

375 g/13 oz. package all-butter puff
    pastry/dough, thawed if frozen
100 g/$\frac{2}{3}$ cup icing/confectioners'
    sugar
caster/granulated sugar, to sprinkle

COCONUT CRÈME DIPLOMAT
200 ml/$\frac{3}{4}$ cup full-fat/whole milk
150 ml/$\frac{2}{3}$ cup coconut milk
$\frac{1}{2}$ vanilla pod/bean
3 egg yolks
50 g/$\frac{1}{4}$ cup caster/superfine sugar
1$\frac{1}{2}$ tablespoons cornflour/cornstarch
1–2 tablespoons Malibu (optional)
250 ml/1 cup double/heavy cream,
    whipped

MACERATED MANGO
1 large or 2 small ripe mangoes
zest and juice of 1 lime

2 baking sheets, lined with
    parchment paper

1 baking sheet

a disposable piping/pastry bag

a cook's blow torch

MAKES 12

Preheat the oven to 180°C fan/
200°C/400°F/Gas 6.

Cut the pastry into three evenly
sized pieces. Roll each piece out
on a lightly floured work surface
into neat 18 x 23-cm/7 x 9-inch
rectangles. Lay clingfilm/plastic
wrap on top of each rectangle and
stack on top of a floured baking
sheet. Chill the pastry in the fridge
for 20 minutes until firm.

Transfer one of the rectangles to
one of the lined baking sheets.
Dust with icing/confectioners'
sugar and lay a sheet of parchment
paper on top. Place an unlined

baking sheet directly on top of
the parchment and bake on the
middle shelf of the preheated
oven for about 12 minutes until
the pastry is golden brown, crisp
and caramelized on top. Bake the
other pastry rectangles in the same
way. Leave to cool completely,
then, using a serrated knife, cut
each rectangle into 7 x 4-cm/
3 x 1½-inch rectangles – you
need 36 in total.

To make the coconut crème
diplomat, heat the milk with the
coconut milk and vanilla pod/bean
in a small pan set over a low heat.

Bring slowly just to the boil, then remove from the heat and leave to infuse for 15 minutes.

Meanwhile, beat the egg yolks with the sugar and cornflour/cornstarch until pale and light.

Remove the vanilla pod/bean and reheat the vanilla-infused milk until just below boiling, then, whisking constantly, pour into the bowl with the egg mixture. Mix until smooth, then return to the pan and, stirring constantly, heat over a low–medium heat until gently boiling and thickened. Add the Malibu, if using, and mix in.

Strain the mixture through a fine-mesh sieve/strainer into a bowl and cover the surface with clingfilm/plastic wrap to prevent a skin forming. Leave until cold, then fold the whipped cream through the mixture and scoop into the piping/pastry bag.

To prepare the mango, remove the skin using a sharp knife and cut the flesh into small dice. Discard the stone. Tip the flesh into a bowl, add the lime zest and juice, mix to combine and leave to macerate for 30 minutes.

Lay 24 of the pastry rectangles on the work surface. Drain the mango from the lime juice. Pipe small bulbs of coconut crème diplomat at each corner of all 24 pastry rectangles. Place a few pieces of diced mango alongside the crème and continue piping crème alternated with mango until the surface of each rectangle is covered like a chequerboard.

Carefully place 12 garnished pastries on a serving plate and top with a second layer. Position the remaining pastry rectangles on top, sprinkle with caster/granulated sugar and flame lightly with a blow torch to brûlée the tops. Serve immediately.

Rose cream religieuses

Religieuse *is the French word for 'nun' and these cute choux buns are said to resemble nuns in their habits.*

BASIC CHOUX PASTRY

65 g/½ cup plain/all-purpose flour

50 g/3½ tablespoons butter, cut into cubes

150 ml/⅔ cup water

1 teaspoon caster/granulated sugar

1 pinch of salt

2 large eggs

ROSE CREAM

2 tablespoons rose syrup

500 ml/2 cups double/heavy cream

FONDANT ICING

1 tablespoon rose syrup

200 g/1⅔ cups powdered fondant icing/confectioners' sugar

pink food colouring

18 silver dragees, to decorate

2 baking sheets, greased and lined with parchment paper

2 piping/pastry bags, fitted with small round nozzles/tips

1 piping/pastry bag, fitted with a very small star nozzle/tip

MAKES 18

To make the basic choux pastry, sift the flour onto a sheet of parchment paper twice to remove any lumps and to add as much air as possible.

Heat the butter in a saucepan with the water, sugar and salt until the butter is melted. As soon as it is melted, remove the pan from the heat and quickly shoot the flour in all in one go. Beat the mixture very hard with a wooden spoon or whisk until the dough forms a ball and no longer sticks to the sides of the pan. Leave to cool for about 5 minutes.

Whisk the eggs in a separate bowl, then beat a small amount at a time into the pastry using a wooden spoon or a balloon whisk. The mixture will form a sticky paste, which holds its shape when you lift the whisk up. Use the pastry as directed in the recipe.

Preheat the oven to 180°C fan/ 200°C/400°F/Gas 6.

Spoon the choux pastry dough into one of the piping/pastry bags fitted with a round nozzle and pipe 18 5-cm/2-inch diameter rings and

18 1-cm/½-inch diameter balls onto the baking sheets. With clean hands wet your finger and smooth down any peaks from the piping so the rings and balls are round. Bake in the preheated oven for 10 minutes, then with a sharp knife cut a small slit into each ring and ball and return to the oven for 3–5 minutes, until crisp. Cool on a wire rack and then cut each in half.

To make the rose cream, add the rose syrup to the cream and whip to stiff peaks using a whisk. Spoon into the second piping bag fitted with a round nozzle and pipe between the choux ring halves and fill the balls. Reserve some of the cream for decoration.

To make the fondant icing, mix together the rose syrup, powdered fondant icing sugar, 1 tablespoon cold water and a drop of food colouring to achieve a pale pink. Using a round-bladed knife, spread the icing over the tops of the rings. Place a choux ball on top of each ring and ice the top of the balls. Put the reserved rose cream in the piping bag fitted with the star nozzle and pipe decorations on the buns, as desired. Top with a silver dragee. Serve immediately or store in the fridge until needed.

Choquettes

These tiny choux buns are light and simple and although they contain no filling, with their crunchy sugar topping, they make a great addition to afternoon tea. It is best to make these buns with a milk choux as they are richer in flavour but you can replace the milk with water if you prefer. Sugar nibs/pearl sugar are available from online baking stores.

65 g/$\frac{1}{2}$ cup plain/all-purpose flour

50 g/3 tablespoons unsalted butter, cut into cubes

75 ml/$\frac{1}{3}$ cup water

75 ml/$\frac{1}{3}$ cup full-fat/whole milk

1 tablespoon caster/granulated sugar

1 tablespoon vanilla bean paste

a pinch of salt

2 eggs

sugar nibs/pearl sugar, for sprinkling

plain chocolate chips (optional)

a piping/pastry bag, fitted with a round nozzle/tip

2 large baking sheets, lined with parchment paper

MAKES 45

Preheat the oven to 180°C fan/200°C/400°F/Gas 6.

Sift the flour twice to remove any lumps. Heat the butter in a saucepan with the water, milk, sugar, vanilla bean paste and salt until the butter is melted. Bring to the boil, then quickly add the sifted flour all in one go and remove from the heat.

Beat hard with a wooden spoon or whisk until the dough forms a ball and no longer sticks to the sides of the pan. Leave to cool for about 5 minutes. Whisk the eggs in a separate bowl, then beat into the pastry, a small amount at a time, using a wooden spoon or whisk. The mixture will form a sticky paste, which holds its shape when you lift the whisk up.

Spoon the choux pastry into the piping/pastry bag and pipe

45 small balls of pastry a small distance apart on the lined baking sheets. With clean hands wet your finger and smooth down any peaks from the piping. Top the pastry with sugar nibs. Sprinkle a little water into the bottom of the oven to create steam, which will help the choux pastry to rise.

Bake each tray in the preheated oven for 10 minutes, then reduce the temperature to 160°C fan/ 180°C/ 350°F/Gas 4 and bake for

a further 10–15 minutes until the pastry is crisp.

Remove from the oven and cut a small slit in each bun straight away to allow steam to escape. Sprinkle a few chocolate chips over the warm buns, if desired – they will melt onto the pastry slightly. Serve the buns warm or cold. The choquettes are best eaten on the day they are made, but can be eaten the following day if stored in an airtight container.

Blackcurrant éclairs

These dainty éclairs are filled with juicy berries and have a tangy blackcurrant icing on top, both of which provide the perfect contrast to the creamy filling.

1 quantity Basic Choux Pastry
(see page 113)

ICING

180 g/1½ cups fondant icing/
confectioners' sugar, sifted

1–2 tablespoons blackcurrant
preserving syrup (see below)

50 g/1½ oz. dark/bittersweet
chocolate, melted

FILLING

350 ml/1½ cups double/heavy cream

290 g/9½ oz blackcurrants preserved
in light syrup, drained but syrup
reserved

a large baking sheet lined with
parchment paper

2 piping/pastry bags, one fitted with
a large round nozzle/tip and one
with a star nozzle/tip

12 paper cases, to serve

MAKES 12

Preheat the oven to 180°C fan/
200°C/400°F/Gas 6.

Spoon the choux pastry into the
piping/pastry bag fitted with one
of the round nozzles/tips and pipe
12 lengths of pastry, about 10 cm/
4 inches long, onto the baking
sheet, a small distance apart. Pat
down any peaks in the pastry using
a clean wet finger. Sprinkle a little
water into the bottom of the oven
to create steam which will help the
choux pastry to rise.

Bake in the oven for 10 minutes,
then reduce the oven temperature
to 160°C fan/180°C/350°F/Gas 4
and bake for 15–20 minutes until
the pastry is crisp. Remove from
the oven and cut a small slit into
each éclair with a sharp knife to
allow any steam to escape. Leave
to cool.

For the icing, whisk together the
icing/confectioners' sugar with the
blackcurrant syrup until you have
a smooth, thick icing. Spread over
the top of the éclairs. Drizzle the

melted chocolate over the éclairs in thin lines using a fork, then leave the icing to set.

When you are ready to serve, whisk the double/heavy cream and 3 tablespoons of the blackcurrant syrup to stiff peaks. Spoon into the piping/pastry bag fitted with the star nozzle/tip. Carefully cut each éclair in half lengthways and pipe a swirled line of the cream into the bottom of each éclair. Place some of the blackcurrants on top of the cream in each éclair. Cover with the iced tops and serve straight away or store in the fridge until needed.

These éclairs are best eaten on the day they are made, although can be eaten the following day if you wish.

Passion fruit éclairs

Chocolate and passion fruit are a super modern combination – the tanginess of the fruit brings the chocolate to life.

❧ ———— • • • ———— ❧

1 quantity Basic Choux Pastry
(see page 113)

MOUSSE

200 g/6½ oz. dark/bittersweet
chocolate, melted

3 passion fruit, skins discarded

100 ml/⅓ cup plus 1 tablespoon
double/heavy cream

2 egg whites

20 g/1½ tablespoons caster/
superfine sugar

ICING & DECORATION

180 g/1½ cups fondant icing/
confectioners' sugar, sifted

2–3 passion fruit, juiced and
seeds removed

50 g/2 oz. dark/bittersweet
chocolate

a baking sheet lined with parchment
paper

2 piping/pastry bags fitted with
large round nozzles/tips

MAKES 12

Begin by preparing the chocolate mousse as it needs time to set. Place the chocolate in a heatproof bowl set over a pan of simmering water until it is all melted. Stir the passion fruit juice, flesh and seeds, and double/heavy cream into the melted chocolate. The seeds of the passion fruit add a crunchy texture to these éclairs but if you are not keen on them, just remove them using a sieve/strainer and add the juice and flesh of the passion fruit to the chocolate mousse, leaving out the seeds.

Whisk the egg whites to stiff peaks, then whisk in the caster/superfine sugar gradually. Fold the egg whites into the chocolate and leave to chill in the fridge for about 3 hours or overnight until set.

Preheat the oven to 180°C fan/200°C/400°F/Gas 6.

Spoon the choux pastry into one of the piping/pastry bags and pipe 12 lines of pastry onto the baking sheet about 10 cm/4 inches in length, a small distance apart. Pat

down any peaks in the pastry using a clean wet finger. Sprinkle a little water into the bottom of the oven to create steam, which will help the choux pastry to rise.

Bake in the oven for 10 minutes, then reduce the oven temperature to 160°C fan/180°C/350°F/Gas 4 and bake for 15–20 minutes until the pastry is crisp. Remove from the oven and cut a small slit into each pastry to allow steam to escape. Leave to cool then cut the éclairs in half lengthways.

For the icing, mix the icing/ confectioners' sugar with the passion fruit juice until you have a smooth icing, adding a little water

if it is too stiff. This will depend on how much juice was released from your fruit so add gradually. Spread the icing over the tops of each éclair. Using a fork, drizzle thin lines of chocolate onto the icing and swirl in with a cocktail stick/ toothpick before the icing sets.

When you are ready to serve, spoon the choux pastry into the other piping/pastry bag and pipe a line of the chocolate passion fruit mousse into the bottom of each éclair. Cover with the iced tops and serve straight away or store in the fridge until needed. The éclairs are best eaten on the day they are made, although can be eaten the following day if you wish.

Cherry crumble Paris-Brests

Topped with a crunchy buttery crumble and filled with cherries
and almond custard, these choux rings are utterly delicious!
Replace the cherries with different pie fillings if you wish –
apple pie filling with vanilla custard works very well.

1 quantity Basic Choux Pastry
  (see page 113)

CRUMBLE MIX
35 g/$\frac{1}{4}$ cup self-raising/rising flour
20 g/4 teaspoons butter
1 tablespoon caster/granulated sugar
icing/confectioners' sugar, for
  dusting (optional)

CRÈME PÂTISSIERE
1 egg and 1 egg yolk
1 heaped tablespoon cornflour/
  cornstarch
60 g/$\frac{1}{3}$ cup minus 1 teaspoon caster/
  superfine or granulated sugar
150 ml/$\frac{2}{3}$ cup double/heavy cream
100 ml/$\frac{1}{3}$ cup plus 1 tablespoon
  full-fat/whole milk
1 teaspoon almond extract

FILLING
100 ml/$\frac{1}{3}$ cup plus 1 tablespoon
  double/heavy cream, to serve
300 g/10 oz (1$\frac{1}{4}$ cups) cherry pie
  filling

a baking sheet, lined with
  parchment paper
2 piping/pastry bags, 1 fitted with
  a round/plain and 1 with a star
  nozzle/tip

MAKES 12

For the crumble topping, place
the flour, butter and sugar in
a bowl and rub together with your
fingertips to fine crumbs. Set aside
until needed.

Preheat the oven to 180°C fan/
200°C/400°F/Gas 6.

Spoon the choux pastry into one
of the piping/pastry bags fitted
with a round nozzle/tip and pipe
12 rings of choux pastry onto the
baking sheet. Pat down any peaks
in the pastry using a clean wet
finger. Sprinkle over the crumble
mix so that the top of each choux
ring is covered lightly. Do not
worry if any crumble falls onto the
sheet. These can be discarded after

baking (or eaten!). Sprinkle a little water into the bottom of the oven to create steam, which will help the choux pastry to rise.

Bake in the preheated oven for 10 minutes, then reduce the oven temperature to 160°C fan/180°C/ 350°F/Gas 4 and bake for a further 10–15 minutes until the pastry is crisp and the crumble mix is golden brown. Remove from the oven and cut a small slit into each pastry to allow steam to escape. Leave to cool.

To make the crème pâtissière, whisk the egg and egg yolk with the cornflour/cornstarch and sugar until very thick and pale yellow in colour. Place the cream, milk and almond extract in a saucepan and bring to the boil. Pour over the egg mixture, whisking all the time. Return to the pan and whisk over a gentle heat until the mixture becomes very thick. Pour into a bowl and leave to cool. Chill in the fridge until needed.

To serve, whip the cream to stiff peaks, then fold in the almond custard. Spoon into the other piping/pastry bag fitted with a star nozzle/tip. Cut each bun in half and fill with custard and a spoonful of the cherry pie filling. Dust with icing/confectioners' sugar to serve, if desired. Serve straight away or store in the fridge.

Violet éclairs

These éclairs are inspired by the confectionery Parma Violets.
If violet flowers are in season, and you are lucky enough to have
them in your garden, why not crystallize them with sugar to
make dainty decorations?

---

1 quantity Basic Choux Pastry
  (see page 113)

crystallized violets, to decorate
  (optional)

ICING

120 g/1 cup fondant icing/
  confectioners' sugar, sifted

1 tablespoon violet syrup or liqueur

purple food colouring

FILLING

300 ml/2¼ cups double/heavy
  cream

1 tablespoon violet syrup or liqueur

a baking sheet, greased and lined
  with parchment paper

2 piping/pastry bags, 1 fitted with
  a large round nozzle/tip and
  1 with a star nozzle/tip

MAKES 12

Preheat the oven to 180°C fan/
200°C/400°F/Gas 6.

Spoon the choux pastry into the
piping/pastry bag fitted with a
round nozzle/tip and pipe 12
lengths of pastry, about 10 cm/
4 inches long onto the baking
sheet, a small distance apart. Pat
down any peaks in the pastry using
a clean wet finger. Sprinkle a little
water into the bottom of the oven
to create steam, which will help
the choux pastry to rise.

Bake in the preheated oven for
10 minutes, then reduce the oven
temperature to 160°C fan/180°C/
350°F/Gas 4 and bake for a further
15–20 minutes until the pastry
is crisp. Remove from the oven and
cut a small slit into each éclair
with a sharp knife to allow steam
to escape. Leave to cool.

Carefully cut each pastry in half
horizontally using a sharp knife.
For the icing, whisk together the
icing/confectioners' sugar and

violet syrup and a few drops of food colouring, if using, adding a few drops of water if necessary, and spread over the tops of the éclairs using a round-bladed knife. Decorate with the crystallized violets and leave to set.

For the filling, whisk together the cream and violet syrup until the cream reaches stiff peaks. Spoon into the piping/pastry bag fitted with a star nozzle/tip and carefully pipe a layer of cream into each éclair. Cover with the iced tops and serve straight away or store in the fridge until needed.

These éclairs are best eaten on the day they are made.

Pistachio religieuses

Pistachios are an exotic nut with a perfumed flavour. Good-quality pistachios have a vibrant green colour and when finely chopped make an elegant topping for these dainty religieuses.

1 quantity Basic Choux Pastry
(see page 113)

FILLING

110 g/¾ cup shelled pistachios
(unsalted)

30 g/2 tablespoons butter

20 g/2½ tablespoons icing/
confectioners' sugar, sifted

400 ml/1⅔ cups double/heavy cream

ICING

150 g/1¼ cups fondant icing/
confectioners' sugar, sifted

green food colouring

a baking sheet, lined with
parchment paper

3 piping/pastry bags, 2 fitted with
round/plain nozzles/tips and
1 with a small star nozzle/tip

MAKES 12

Preheat the oven to 180°C fan/
200°C/400°F/Gas 6.

Spoon the choux pastry into a piping bag fitted with a round/plain nozzle/tip and pipe 12 rings about 5 cm/2 inches in diameter and 12 small balls of choux pastry onto the lined baking sheet. Pat down any peaks in the pastry using a clean wet finger. Sprinkle a little water into the bottom of the oven to create steam, which will help the choux pastry to rise.

Bake in the preheated oven for 10 minutes, then reduce the oven temperature to 160°C fan/180°C/ 350°F/Gas 4 and bake for a further 15–20 minutes until the pastry is crisp. Remove from the oven and cut a small slit into each pastry to allow steam to escape. Leave to cool completely.

Reserve 12 whole pistachios for decoration, then blitz the remainder to very fine crumbs in a food processor or blender. Remove 3 tablespoons of the ground pistachios for decoration, then add the butter and icing/confectioners' sugar to the blender and blitz to a smooth paste to make pistachio butter.

Whip the cream to stiff peaks. Remove a quarter of the cream and store in the fridge until you are ready to decorate.

Make two small holes in the base of each ring, one on either side, and one small hole in each ball using a sharp knife.

Fold the pistachio butter into the cream and spoon into a piping/pastry bag fitted with a round/plain nozzle/tip. Pipe the cream into each ring and ball, piping through both holes on the ring to make sure that they are generously and evenly filled.

For the icing, mix the icing/confectioners' sugar and food colouring with 1–2 tablespoons of cold water until you have a smooth thick icing. Spread some icing over each ring and sprinkle with the reserved chopped pistachios. Place one of the balls on top of each ring fixed in place with the icing and spread a little icing over the small balls. Place a whole pistachio on top.

Spoon the reserved cream into the piping/pastry bag fitted with a small star nozzle/tip and pipe small stars of cream onto the buns to decorate. Serve straight away or store in the fridge until needed. These buns are best eaten on the day they are made, although can be eaten the following day if you wish.

Caramel Paris-Brests

Traditional Paris-Brests – classic choux rings – are made with coffee, but this version has a rich whiskey cream liqueur filling.

1 quantity Basic Choux Pastry
(see page 113)

FILLING

1 tablespoon Bailey's or other
whiskey cream liqueur

300 ml/1¼ cups double/heavy cream

ICING

200 g/1⅔ cups powdered fondant
icing/confectioners' sugar

2 tablespoons caramel sauce

caramel curls, to decorate

2 baking sheets, greased and lined
with parchment paper

2 piping/pastry bags, both fitted
with round nozzles/tips

MAKES 18

• • •

Preheat the oven to 180°C fan/
200°C/400°F/Gas 6.

Spoon the choux pastry dough into
one of the piping/pastry bags and
pipe 18 rings 6 cm/2½ inch in
diameter a small distance apart on
the lined baking sheets. With clean
hands wet your finger and smooth
down any peaks from the piping so
that the rings are round. Bake in
the preheated oven for 10 minutes,
then with a sharp knife cut a small
slit into each ring and return to the
oven for 3–5 minutes until crisp.
Cool on a wire rack, then slice each
in half horizontally.

To make the cream filling, add the
liqueur to the cream and whip to
stiff peaks using a whisk. Spoon
into the second piping/pastry bag
and pipe balls of cream between
the choux ring halves.

To make the caramel fondant
icing, mix 2 tablespoons cold
water with the fondant icing/
confectioners' sugar and the
caramel sauce until you have
a smooth thick icing. Using a
round-bladed knife, spread the
icing over the tops of the rings
and decorate with caramel curls.

Serve immediately or store in the
fridge until needed.

Praline & coffee éclairs

French pâtisserie has a natural home on the tea table, and these baby éclairs give you a perfect excuse to dig out your cake forks. Each one is just a couple of mouthfuls and they look divine piled up on an elegant cake stand. Filled with a hazelnut praline cream and topped with coffee icing, it's very hard to eat just one!

◦ ◦ ◦

75 g/½ cup plus 1 tablespoon plain/
    all-purpose flour
60 ml/¼ cup full-fat/whole milk
60 ml/¼ cup water
50 g/3 tablespoons butter, diced
a pinch of salt
2 eggs

PRALINE FILLING
50 g/¼ cup caster/granulated sugar
50 g/⅓ cup blanched hazelnuts,
    chopped
120 ml/½ cup whipping cream

ICING
25 g/2 tablespoons unsalted butter
1 teaspoon instant coffee, dissolved
    in 3 tablespoons boiling water
200 g/1 cup icing/confectioners'
    sugar, sifted

3 baking sheets, 1 lightly greased
    and 2 lined with parchment paper
a piping/pastry bag, fitted with
    a 1–1.5-cm/½–¾-inch round
    nozzle/tip

MAKES ABOUT 20

First make the praline. Heat the sugar in a dry saucepan over a medium heat, stirring, for about 5 minutes until dissolved and pale gold. Add the hazelnuts and cook, stirring, for about 1 minute, then pour onto the greased baking sheet and let harden for at least 20 minutes.

Preheat the oven to 200°C fan/220°C/425°F/Gas 7.

Sift the flour onto a sheet of parchment paper. Heat the milk, water, butter and salt in a saucepan and bring to the boil for 1 minute. Remove from the heat and, stirring, shoot the flour into the pan all at once. When the mixture becomes smooth, return to the heat, stirring constantly, for about 1 minute. Remove from the heat again and beat in the eggs, one at a time, until the mixture is smooth and glossy.

Spoon the mixture into the piping/pastry bag and pipe 5–6-cm/2-inch fingers of the mixture onto the lined baking sheets. Bake in the preheated oven for about 12 minutes until golden. Transfer to a wire rack and cut a slit in the side of each one to let any steam escape. Let cool completely.

To make the filling, put the hardened praline in a food processor and process briefly to crush. Whip the cream until stiff, then fold in the crushed praline. Using the piping/pastry bag, fill the éclairs with the cream.

To make the coffee icing, put the butter and dissolved coffee in a heatproof bowl and set over a saucepan of simmering water until melted. Add the icing/confectioners' sugar and stir for about 4 minutes until smooth and glossy. Spoon the icing over the éclairs immediately and serve.

Lemon & lime meringue tartlets

Surprisingly simple to make, these tartlets use a sablé sweet pastry or pâte sablée, *which can be quickly made in a food processor, with an Italian meringue topping, which you will need a thermometer for.*

PÂTE SABLÉE PASTRY

200 g/1½ cups plain/all-purpose flour

100 g/7 tablespoons butter, at room temperature

20 g/scant ¼ cup ground almonds

60 g/7 tablespoons icing/confectioners' sugar, plus extra for dusting

1 egg yolk

FILLING

2 eggs

1 egg yolk

30 g/2½ tablespoons caster/granulated sugar

150 ml/⅔ cup double/heavy cream

grated zest and freshly squeezed juice of 1 lemon

grated zest and freshly squeezed juice of 1 lime

MERINGUE

2 egg whites

½ teaspoon vanilla extract

75 g/6 tablespoons caster/granulated sugar

6 small fluted tartlet pans or rings

a sugar thermometer

a cook's blow torch

MAKES 6

For the pastry, blitz the flour, butter and almonds together in a food processor before adding the icing/confectioners' sugar, then the egg yolk. Continue to blitz until it forms a ball. Roll out the pastry to a thickness of about 2 cm/¾ inch. Wrap it in some clingfilm/plastic wrap and place in the fridge for an hour to chill.

Once the pastry is chilled, divide into six and roll each of these out to a thickness of about 3 mm/ ⅛ inch (dust the pastry with a little icing/confectioners' sugar to stop it sticking). Place the pastry into the small tartlet pans or rings, covering the base and sides. Place the tartlet bases in the fridge for a further 30 minutes.

Preheat the oven to 140°C fan/ 160°C/325°F/Gas 3.

Prick the tartlet bases with a fork to stop them rising and bake in the preheated oven for 10 minutes to 'set' the pastry; it should be just cooked but still pale.

To make the tartlet filling, whisk the eggs, egg yolk, sugar, cream, and juice and zest of the lemon and lime together, before carefully pouring into the tartlet bases. Bake the filled bases in the preheated oven for 7–9 minutes. Check after 7 minutes to see whether the mix has just set – it should still wobble a little when shaken.

To make the meringue, you will need a spotlessly clean mixing bowl (wipe around the inside with a little vinegar or lemon juice to remove any oil, which will stop the meringue from setting firm).

Whisk the egg whites and vanilla extract to soft peaks.

Next, make a sugar syrup. In a heavy-bottomed saucepan, add enough water to just cover the base, then add the sugar and heat until the mixture is boiling and the temperature reaches 115°C/240°F.

Now, while continuing to whisk the egg whites, pour the hot sugar syrup in a slow stream into the mixing bowl. Keep whisking until firm peaks are formed. Spoon or pipe the Italian meringue onto the tartlets and use a blow torch to caramelize it. Serve as they are, or gently warmed for 10 minutes in a very low oven to make them extra special.

Meringue nests

Crisp on the outside and chewy in the middle, meringue nests are so versatile. Their sweet simplicity of flavour combines so well with fresh fruit and whipped cream.

* * *

3 egg whites
$\frac{1}{2}$ teaspoon white vinegar
$\frac{1}{4}$ teaspoon vanilla extract
180g/1 cup caster/superfine sugar

TOPPING
600 ml/2$\frac{1}{2}$ cups whipping cream
30 g/3 tablespoons caster/superfine
  sugar
fresh fruit of choice

2 baking sheets, lined with
  parchment paper

MAKES ABOUT 20

• • •

Preheat the oven to 90°C fan/
110°C/225°F/Gas $\frac{1}{4}$.

Put the egg whites, vinegar and vanilla extract into a large, clean, grease-free bowl and whisk on high speed with an electric hand whisk until the mixture has doubled in volume and stiff peaks are formed. Add about a third of the sugar and beat on high speed for 5 minutes until all the sugar is dissolved.

Repeat this process, adding the sugar a third at a time and beating for 5 minutes between each addition. The mixture should become stiff.

Scoop spoonfuls of the mixture onto the prepared baking sheets to form mounds of the desired size. Make a dip in each one with the spoon to form a nest shape. Bake the meringues in the preheated oven for about 60–80 minutes or until they sound crispy and hollow when tapped underneath. Turn off the oven and leave them to cool in the oven with the door ajar for about 30 minutes. Remove from the oven and transfer to a wire rack to cool completely.

To serve, whip the cream and sugar with an electric hand whisk until soft peaks are formed. Serve the meringue nests topped with whipped cream and fresh fruit.

The meringues will keep for 14 days in an airtight container, or can be frozen for up to 2 months.

Pink meringue kisses

Dehydrated raspberries have a lovely sharpness that offsets sweet meringue and cream perfectly in these delicate kisses.

RASPBERRIES

200 g/1½ cups raspberries

freshly squeezed juice of ½ lemon

or

40 g/1½ oz. dehydrated raspberry powder

MERINGUES

200 g/1 cup caster/superfine sugar

100 g/½ cup egg whites (approx. 3 large/US extra-large eggs)

BUTTERCREAM

50 g/3½ tablespoons butter, softened

100 g/¾ cup icing/confectioners' sugar

1 teaspoon vanilla extract

a piping/pastry bag

2 baking sheets, lined with parchment paper

MAKES 19

For the raspberries (if using fresh raspberries), preheat the oven to 70°C fan/90°C/195°F/the lowest gas setting.

Place a sheet of parchment paper over a wire rack. Spread the raspberries over the parchment and sprinkle with the lemon juice. Place in the preheated oven and leave in the oven overnight, or for at least 8 hours. Once dried, blitz the raspberries in a food processor until they form a fine powder, then pass them through a sieve/strainer.

For the meringues, preheat the oven to 180°C fan/200°C/400°F/ Gas 6. Ensure the bowl you use is perfectly clean. Sprinkle the sugar over a non-stick baking sheet and place into the preheated oven. Place the egg whites in a stand mixer fitted with a balloon whisk (or use a mixing bowl and a hand-held electric whisk) and start mixing until stiff peaks form; this will take 5–8 minutes. Remove the, now hot, sugar from the oven and turn the oven down to 80°C fan/ 100°C/ 210°F/Gas ¼ .

Add about one-quarter of the sugar to the egg white mix. Whisk for a couple of minutes, then repeat until all the sugar has been combined. Whisk for another 5 minutes, checking that the mixture is fully combined and that no graininess remains. Finally, add about three-quarters of the raspberry powder and fold together, but leave some patterns in the mixture.

Spoon the meringue mixture into the piping/pastry bag and snip off the tip. Pipe the meringue mixture onto the lined baking sheets, making 24–26 kisses, each about 5-cm/2-inch. Bake in the preheated oven for 45 minutes. Check the outer layer of meringue has fully cooked and is crispy; continue cooking in 10-minute intervals if not. Switch the oven off and leave the meringues to cool in the oven for at least 30 minutes. Store the meringues in an airtight container until you are ready to serve.

For the buttercream, in a mixing bowl, whisk the butter and icing/confectioners' sugar together to form a smooth cream. Add the vanilla and 4–5 teaspoons of water. Whisk until a smooth, light buttercream is made. To serve, place a teaspoon of the buttercream onto the flat side of one meringue and stick it to the flat side of another. Sprinkle a little of the remaining raspberry powder over the top to decorate.

Tea voyage macarons

A bite of these macarons will transport you to the other end of the world and fill you with zen-like contentment. The green tea and jasmine extract make this a perfect option for a tea party.

GREEN TEA GANACHE

100 ml/⅓ cup plus 1 tablespoon single/light cream

50 g/2 oz. mascarpone

300 g/10½ oz. white chocolate, chopped

1 teaspoon butter

1 teaspoon matcha (green tea) powder

2 drops of pure jasmine extract

VANILLA MACARON SHELLS

240 g/1¾ cups icing/confectioners' sugar

140 g/1½ cups ground almonds

½ vanilla pod/bean

5 egg whites

50 g/¼ cup caster/superfine sugar

finely chopped pistachios, to sprinkle

a piping/pastry bag, fitted with a plain nozzle/tip

baking sheets lined with parchment paper

MAKES ABOUT 25

To make the green tea ganache, start the day before you want to bake the macarons. Put the cream and mascarpone in a saucepan and gently bring to the boil. Add the chocolate and butter and stir until melted. Remove from the heat and whisk with an electric whisk until smooth. Stir in the matcha powder and jasmine extract. Cover and refrigerate for 24 hours.

The next day, preheat the oven to 125°C fan/145°C/275°F/Gas 1. Bring the ganache to room temperature.

To make the vanilla macaron shells, sift the icing/confectioners' sugar into a food processor, add the almonds and blitz thoroughly. Split the vanilla pod/bean lengthways and scrape the seeds out into a grease-free mixing bowl. Add the egg whites and whisk with an electric whisk until stiff peaks form. Gradually add the sugar, whisking until all the sugar is used up and the egg whites are glossy.

Fold the blitzed sugar/almonds into the egg whites until well combined and smooth. Fill the piping/pastry bag with the mixture and pipe neat 4-cm/1½-inch rounds on the prepared baking sheets. Space the rounds 3 cm/ 1¼ inches apart. Sprinkle a tiny amount of finely chopped pistachios on top of each round – not too much otherwise the macarons won't rise. Allow to set for 30–60 minutes until a skin forms – you should be able to touch the surface of the macarons very gently with a wet finger without sticking to them.

Bake in the preheated oven for about 12 minutes. Allow to cool on the baking sheet.

Fill the piping/pastry bag with the ganache and pipe some onto the flat underside of half of the cold macarons. Sandwich with another macaron shell.

Rhubarb & custard macarons

An all-time favourite flavour combination! Is it rhubarb crumble with custard or those classic boiled sweets/hard candies that are to blame? Either way, these double-filled macarons will certainly make you feel nostalgic!

175 g/1¾ cups ground almonds

175 g/1¼ cups icing/confectioners' sugar

150 g/scant ¾ cup egg whites (about 4 egg whites)

200 g/1 cup caster/superfine sugar

1 teaspoon vanilla extract

pink food colouring paste

4 tablespoons rhubarb jam/jelly

red food colouring, to decorate

BUTTERCREAM

150 g/1 stick plus 2 tablespoons butter, softened

300 g/2 cups icing/confectioners' sugar

1 teaspoon custard powder

1 teaspoon vanilla extract

2 large baking sheets, lined with parchment paper

a large piping/pastry bag, fitted with a 1-cm/3/8-inch plain nozzle/tip

2 disposable piping/pastry bags

MAKES 30

Combine the ground almonds and icing/confectioners' sugar in a food processor and blitz for up to 1 minute to finely grind and thoroughly mix. Tip into a mixing bowl, add 50 g/scant ¼ cup of the egg whites and beat until combined into a thick paste. Set aside.

Fill a medium-sized saucepan with water and bring to a gentle simmer. Tip the remaining egg whites into a medium heatproof bowl, add the caster/superfine sugar and set the bowl over the simmering water, ensuring that it does not touch the water. Slowly beat the egg whites and sugar with a handheld electric whisk until combined, continuing to whisk for about 3 minutes until the sugar has completely dissolved and the mixture is a thick glossy, bright white meringue. Remove the bowl from the pan and continue to whisk on medium–fast speed for another 3 minutes until cool and very thick.

With a large metal spoon or rubber spatula, fold in the vanilla extract and food colouring in tiny amounts – you can add more but you can't take any away.

Add one-quarter of the meringue to the almond paste, stirring well to loosen and combine the mixture. Fold this back into the meringue and mix until well combined and resembling thick molten lava that will hold a ribbon trail for about 5 seconds.

Working quickly, scoop the mixture into a large piping/pastry bag and pipe 30 neat 4-cm/ $1\frac{1}{2}$-inch round macarons onto each lined baking sheet. Set aside for about 30 minutes until the macarons have firmed up and a light skin has formed on the surface.

Preheat the oven to 140°C fan/ 160°C/325°F/Gas 3.

Bake the macarons, one sheet at a time, on the middle shelf of the preheated oven for 10–12 minutes until well risen and crisp on top. Remove and allow to cool completely on the sheets.

Meanwhile, prepare the buttercream filling. Beat the butter until really pale and light. Gradually add the sugar in 3 or 4 batches and mix until smooth. Add the custard powder and vanilla extract and combine thoroughly. Scoop the buttercream into a disposable piping/pastry bag and snip the end into a $\frac{1}{2}$–1 cm/ $\frac{1}{4}$–$\frac{1}{2}$ inch nozzle.

Turn half of the macarons upside down and pipe the buttercream in a ring around the edge of the flat surface. Fill the hole in the middle of the ring with rhubarb jam/jelly and sandwich with the remaining macaron shells. Brush with red food colouring and serve.

Raspberry macarons

A similarly vibrant colour to the rhubarb and custard macarons on the previous page, but with a very different flavour, these raspberry macarons are very moreish. It's almost impossible to eat just one where there is a cake stand piled high with them in front of you! Choose a good-quality raspberry jam/jelly which is not too runny, otherwise the filling may ooze out when you bite into the macarons.

220 g/1¾ cups icing/confectioners' sugar

160 g/1⅓ cups ground almonds

4 large egg whites

a pinch of salt

95 g/½ cup caster/superfine sugar

red food colouring gel

200 g/¾ cup high fruit-content raspberry jam/jelly

2 or 3 baking sheets, lined with parchment paper

a piping/pastry bag

MAKES ABOUT 30

Blitz the icing/confectioners' sugar and almonds in a food processor until very fine, then push the mixture through a fine-meshed sieve/strainer. Set aside.

Whisk the egg whites and salt together until stiff and glossy. Add the sugar mixture, one-third at a time, beating again each time, until the eggs are stiff and glossy and all the sugar has been incorporated.

Carefully but thoroughly fold the almond mixture into the egg whites, until fully incorporated but still light. Fold in enough food colouring to achieve the desired pink colour.

Spoon the mixture into a large piping/pastry bag and pipe neat 4-cm/1½-inch rounds onto the lined baking sheets. When all the macarons have been piped, take hold of the baking sheet and tap it firmly on the work surface 2 or 3 times to knock out any air bubbles.

Preheat the oven to 120°C fan/ 140°C/275°F/Gas ½ and leave the baking sheets to stand for 30 minutes.

Bake the macarons in the preheated oven for about 15 minutes, until the shells are crisp and they have grown little 'feet'. Remove from the oven and leave to cool.

Once completely cool, sandwich together with the raspberry jam/ jelly and serve.

Dark chocolate, prune & Armagnac mousses

The white chocolate cases are a bit fiddly to make, but the end result of these creamy, luscious mousses is so divine that it's worth every minute of preparation. They are quite rich, so serve alongside a plate of delicate tuiles and perhaps a simple, old-fashioned fruit cake (see page 160).

※ ─── • • • ─── ※

140 g/5 oz. white chocolate, melted and cooled, plus extra shavings to decorate

5 ready-to-eat pitted/stoned prunes

1 tablespoon Armagnac

60 g/2 oz. dark/bittersweet chocolate (70–80% cocoa solids)

$\frac{1}{2}$ tablespoon butter

$1\frac{1}{2}$ tablespoons double/heavy cream

1 egg, separated

frosted edible flower petals, to decorate (optional)

a thin sheet of Cellophane

sticky tape

a baking sheet, lined with parchment paper

MAKES 8

Cut out eight 4 x 15-cm/$1\frac{3}{4}$ x 6-inch strips of Cellophane, coil each one to make a collar, about 4 cm/$1\frac{3}{4}$ inches in diameter, and secure with sticky tape. Stand the collars on the prepared baking sheet.

Using a teaspoon, coat the inside of each collar with the melted white chocolate, leaving the top ragged and smeared. Drop a spoonful of chocolate into the bottom of each collar and spread out to form a base. Chill for about 15 minutes, then remove from the fridge and add a little more chocolate to any thin patches so that there's a good layer of chocolate all round. Return to the fridge and chill for at least 30 minutes.

Put the prunes, Armagnac and 2 tablespoons water in a food processor and blend to make a smooth purée.

Put the dark/bittersweet chocolate in a heatproof bowl and set over a saucepan of simmering water until melted. Alternatively, melt the chocolate in a microwave. Remove from the heat and stir in the butter until melted, then stir in the prune purée, cream and egg yolk.

Put the egg white in a clean bowl and whisk to form stiff peaks. Fold a spoonful into the chocolate mixture, then fold in the remaining egg white, one-third at a time. Carefully spoon 1½–2 tablespoons of the mousse into each white chocolate case and chill in the fridge for at least 2 hours.

To serve, carefully remove the sticky tape and unpeel the collars. Arrange on a serving plate using a spatula to transfer them, and decorate with shavings of white chocolate or frosted edible flower petals, if liked.

Individual no-bake cookie butter cheesecakes

No-bake cheesecakes are the ideal way to get your cheesecake fix without the need for baking. Cookie butter works brilliantly to flavour this cheesecake and is also delicious eaten with a spoon directly from the jar!

❦ — • • • — ❦

100 g/3½ oz. cookies (digestive biscuits/Graham crackers work well)

25 g/1¾ tablespoons unsalted butter

½ teaspoon ground cinnamon

1 teaspoon light brown sugar

350 g/1¾ cups full-fat cream cheese

200 g/1 cup cookie butter, such as Biscoff or Speculoos

150 ml/¾ cup double/heavy cream

80 g/½ cup icing/confectioners' sugar, sifted

TO SERVE

4 whole cookies (optional)

cookie crumbs (optional)

4 glass sundae glasses or ramekins

MAKES 4

In a food processor, blitz the cookies until they resemble fine breadcrumbs. Alternatively, put them in a food bag, wrap in a clean kitchen cloth and bash with the end of a rolling pin.

Melt the butter in the microwave for 20–30 seconds at 800W.

Pour the melted butter, cinnamon and light brown sugar into the food processor with the cookie crumbs and pulse until all of the cookie crumbs are wet. Alternatively, mix well with a wooden spoon in a mixing bowl.

Spoon the cookie crumbs into the serving glasses, so that each has an equal amount. Use a teaspoon to push the crumbs in and to give them a flat surface.

Into the bowl of a stand mixer with a whisk attachment, or a mixing bowl using a handheld electric whisk, empty in the cream cheese and cookie butter and whip until fully combined and pale. Pour in the cream and sifted icing/confectioners' sugar and whip again on a medium speed for 2–3 minutes until thickened.

Divide the cheesecake mixture evenly between the cookie bases, so that each has an equal amount, and swirl the top, then put in the fridge for at least 3 hours (or overnight).

Just before serving, top with a whole cookie and/or cookie crumbs. These cheesecakes should be stored in the fridge and eaten within 3 days.

White chocolate
& raspberry cheesecake bites

*Rich, creamy cheesecake is always a favourite. Served in tiny
squares and topped with a gilded raspberry, it is sure to delight.*

BASE
180 g/6 oz. butter shortcake cookies
70 g/5 tablespoons butter, melted

TOPPING
200 ml/¾ cup crème fraîche or
    sour cream
200 g/¾ cup mascarpone
100 g/3½ oz. white chocolate,
    melted and cooled
100 g/¾ cup raspberries

TO ASSEMBLE
20 raspberries
golden/light corn syrup
gold leaf

a 20 x 15-cm/8 x 6-inch loose-based
    baking pan, greased and lined

MAKES 20

To make the base, put the cookies in
a food processor and blitz to a fine
crumb. Transfer to a bowl, pour in
the melted butter and mix together.
Spoon the cookie base into the
prepared pan and press down firmly
with the back of a spoon.

To make the cheesecake topping,
whisk together the crème fraîche
and mascarpone. Fold in the cooled
melted chocolate and raspberries
with a spatula and spoon the
mixture into the pan. Level the
surface of the cheesecake with
a spatula and chill in the fridge
for 3 hours, until set.

When you are ready to serve, remove
the cheesecake from the pan. Cut
into 20 squares, using a sharp knife.
Place a raspberry in the middle of
each square and use a pastry brush
to brush the tip with a little golden/
corn syrup. Decorate with gold leaf
by pressing it into the syrup. Serve
immediately or store in the fridge
until needed.

Crème brûlée spoons

These spoon-sized versions of crème brûlée are just the perfect accompaniment to an afternoon tea. A little lemon juice in the crème brûlée reduces the sweetness and helps them to set.

150 ml/⅔ cup double/heavy cream

1 egg

1 egg yolk

50 g/¼ cup caster/granulated sugar,
plus extra for topping

freshly squeezed juice of ½ lemon

12 deep china spoons

a cook's blow torch

MAKES 12

In a heavy-bottomed saucepan, heat the cream over a low heat, gently stirring, until it is just simmering, then take it immediately off the heat.

In a mixing bowl, whisk together the egg, egg yolk and sugar to form a paste. Pour the hot cream into the mixing bowl, continuously whisking to combine into a custard, before finally adding the lemon juice.

Now return the custard to the saucepan and carefully, over a low heat, so as not to catch or burn it, whisk the custard over the heat until it is thickened.

Spoon the custard evenly into the serving spoons while it is hot and tap them to level the custard and remove any air bubbles. Place the serving spoons in the fridge for at least 1 hour to chill.

To serve, sprinkle enough sugar over each spoonful of custard to cover it. Using a blow torch, caramelize the sugar, forming a hard surface of caramel on top.

Chapter 5

Larger Cakes
& Teatime Tarts

Victoria sandwich

This easy recipe for the classic afternoon cake uses the 'all-in' method of mixing flour, butter, sugar and eggs, but it does require super fresh eggs.

━━━━━ ❖ • • • ❖ ━━━━━

5 eggs

approx. 250 g/scant 2 cups self-raising/rising flour

approx. 250 g/2¼ sticks butter, softened

approx. 250 g/1¼ cups caster/granulated sugar

1 teaspoon vanilla extract

STRAWBERRIES & CREAM FILLING

200 g/2 cups fresh strawberries

freshly squeezed juice of 1 lemon

50 g/¼ cup caster/granulated sugar

300 ml/1¼ cups whipping cream

50 g/6 tablespoons icing/confectioners' sugar, plus extra for dusting

1 teaspoon vanilla extract

2 x 25-cm/10-inch round cake pans, lightly oiled and lined with parchment paper (single layer on the base and a double/folded layer around the sides)

a cook's thermometer

SERVES 10

Preheat the oven to 120°C fan/140°C/280°F/Gas 1.

Place a mixing bowl onto some scales and zero the scales. Into the bowl, crack the eggs and make a note of the weight. Add the same weight of flour, softened butter and caster/granulated sugar.

Mix for a few minutes using a hand-held electric whisk or in a stand mixer until it just forms a smooth batter. Add the vanilla extract and mix for another minute to combine.

Divide the mixture between the two lined cake pans, then place in the preheated oven for 25–30 minutes. Do not open your oven for any reason for at least 20 minutes, or the cakes may collapse! The cakes are cooked when a skewer poked into the centre comes out clean and the internal temperature reaches 90°C/195°F. Remove from the oven immediately when this temperature is reached, so the cakes don't dry out.

Leave the cakes to cool for about 20 minutes before removing from the pans as this will complete the baking but keep the cakes moist. Transfer to a wire rack to cool completely.

For the filling, chop the berries into small pieces and place in a mixing bowl with the lemon juice and caster/granulated sugar. Mix together and leave for at least 20 minutes before filling on the cake.

Whip the cream, icing/confectioners' sugar and vanilla extract together until it forms, and holds, soft peaks.

Level the top, if necessary, of one of the cakes using a bread knife. Place the strawberries on the levelled top. Turn the other half over and spread the cream generously on the flat side. Place the top, cream-side down, onto the strawberry-coated half. Dust with icing/confectioners' sugar.

Fruit cake

A good fruit cake takes time, and alcohol. Soaking the dried fruit overnight in brandy and 'feeding' the baked cake gives this classic a naughty but delicious flavour. It is important to line the cake pan as directed, to stop the cake drying out during baking.

200 g/scant 1½ cups sultanas/ golden raisins

200 g/scant 1½ cups (dark) raisins

50 g/generous ⅓ cup dried mixed peel

200 g/1½ cups pitted/stoned dates, chopped

200 ml/generous ¾ cup brandy

250 g/1¼ cups demerara sugar

250 g/2¼ sticks butter, softened

4 eggs

200 g/1½ cups self-raising/ rising flour

50 g/½ cup ground almonds

grated zest of 1 lemon

1 teaspoon vanilla extract

a 30-cm/12-inch round cake pan, buttered and lined with parchment paper (to stop the edges drying out, add two further layers of paper on the outside of the pan, which rise above the top of the tin by at least 2.5 cm/ 1 inch; tie the outer layers of paper with cooking twine to hold in place)

a cook's thermometer

SERVES 10

The night before, place the sultanas/golden raisins, raisins, mixed peel and chopped dates in a container and cover them with the brandy.

The next day, preheat the oven to 100°C fan/120°C/250°F/Gas 1.

Place the sugar and butter in a large bowl. Whisk with a hand-held electric whisk until the mixture is creamy and has increased in volume by about half. Add the eggs, one at a time, and 2 teaspoons of the flour, and continue whisking until a smooth mixture is formed.

Add the remaining flour and ground almonds and fold together.

Add the lemon zest and the vanilla extract whilst continuing to fold together. Finally, drain the soaked fruit (reserving the brandy and setting it aside for later), and add the fruit to the mixture. Fold together to combine thoroughly.

Pour the mixture into the prepared cake pan. Bake in the preheated oven for $2\frac{1}{2}$ hours, until a skewer poked into the centre comes out clean and the internal temperature reaches 95°C/205°F.

Remove carefully from the oven and leave to cool for at least 30 minutes before removing from the cake pan. Transfer to a wire rack and cool completely.

Wrap the cold cake, first in parchment paper, and then in a layer of foil. Poke small holes in the top of the cake and pour over the reserved brandy before sealing with foil.

Leave in the fridge overnight before serving.

Apple Bourbon pecan cake

Juicy chunks of apple, perfectly spiced with a warming combination of cinnamon, nutmeg, ginger, cardamom, allspice and cloves, this cake is packed with luscious flavour. Try a slice at breakfast time, too – that is if there's any leftover from your afternoon tea!

225 g/2 sticks unsalted butter, softened

220 g/1 cup plus 1 tablespoon caster/granulated sugar

220 g/1 cup plus 1 tablespoon dark brown soft sugar

3 eggs

280 g/2 cups plain/all-purpose flour

1 teaspoon baking powder

½ teaspoon bicarbonate of soda/baking soda

1 teaspoon ground allspice

1½ teaspoons ground cinnamon

1 teaspoon freshly grated nutmeg

¼ teaspoon ground cloves

¼ teaspoon ground ginger

¼ teaspoon ground cardamom

½ teaspoon salt

3 tablespoons Bourbon

3 Granny Smith apples, peeled, cored and cut into chunks

120 g/1 cup shelled whole pecans, toasted and roughly chopped

a 20-cm/8-inch round cake pan, greased and baselined with parchment paper

SERVES 8 12

Preheat the oven to 140°C fan/160°C/315°F/Gas 3.

Using an electric mixer with paddle or beater attachment (or an electric whisk), beat the butter and both sugars until the mixture is almost light in colour and fluffy in texture. Add the eggs, one at a time, beating until thoroughly combined before adding the next. Scrape down the side of the bowl and mix again for 1 minute.

In another bowl, combine the flour, baking powder, bicarbonate of soda/baking soda, all the spices and salt and sift twice.

Add one-third of the flour mixture to the egg mixture and mix until well incorporated. Repeat with another third of the flour mixture, then the rest of the flour mixture and mix until just combined.

Pour the Bourbon over the apples in a bowl and mix. Fold the apples and pecans into the cake mixture. Spoon the mixture into the prepared cake pan.

Bake in the preheated oven for 55–70 minutes. A wooden skewer inserted in the middle should come out with almost no crumbs attached, and the middle of the cake, when pressed, should spring back slightly instead of sink. Bake for an additional 5–10 minutes if necessary.

Remove from the oven and let cool in the pan for 10 minutes. Slide a table knife all around the edge to loosen the cake, then remove from the pan. Transfer to a wire rack to cool for 1 hour.

Hummingbird cake

Hummingbird cake is one of those classic Southern confections where you combine the most incongruous tropical items – pineapple, coconut and bananas – and create a homey American classic. The addition of cardamom and rum make it just a touch more tropical. Choose pineapple pieces in light syrup rather than fruit juice, as it needs that sugar push to make it a proper hummingbird cake. You may have some of the cream cheese icing leftover, but it can be used for other cakes or desserts.

3 eggs

300 g/1½ cups caster/granulated sugar

140 g/⅔ cup light brown soft sugar

250 ml/1 cup sunflower oil

425 g/3 cups plain/all-purpose flour

½ teaspoon freshly grated nutmeg

¼ teaspoon ground allspice

1 teaspoon ground cinnamon

½ teaspoon ground cardamom

1 teaspoon bicarbonate of soda/ baking soda

250 g/9 oz. chopped banana (from about 3–4 bananas)

225 g/8 oz. canned pineapple pieces in light syrup, drained well

100 g/1 cup soft shredded coconut e.g. Baker's Angel Flake (do not replace with desiccated coconut)

100 g/¾ cup shelled pecans, crushed, plus about 150 g/1 cup, crushed, to decorate

1 tablespoon dark rum

CREAM CHEESE ICING

180 g/1½ sticks butter, softened

250 g/2¼ cups icing/confectioners' sugar

2 tablespoons golden/light corn syrup

800 g/1 lb. 2 oz. full-fat cream cheese

2 teaspoons vanilla extract

a 23-cm/9-inch round cake pan, greased and baselined with parchment paper

SERVES 8–12

Preheat the oven to 140°C fan/ 160°C/315°F/Gas 4.

Using an electric mixer with paddle or beater attachment (or an electric whisk), whisk the eggs and both sugars together. While whisking, add the oil in a steady stream until fully combined.

In another bowl, combine the flour, all the spices and the bicarbonate of soda/baking soda and sift twice.

Add the flour mixture to the egg mixture and mix slowly until just combined. Add the bananas, pineapple pieces, coconut and pecans and mix until well combined. Stir in the rum.

Spoon the mixture into the prepared cake pan. Bake in the preheated oven for 50–60 minutes. A wooden skewer inserted in the middle should come out with almost no crumbs attached, and the middle of the cake, when pressed, should spring back slightly instead of sink. Bake for an additional 5–10 minutes if necessary.

Remove from the oven and let cool in the pan for 10 minutes. Slide a table knife all around the edge to loosen the cake, then remove from the pan. Transfer to a wire rack to cool for 1 hour.

To make the cream cheese icing, in a bowl beat the butter and sugar together to a smooth consistency. Add the cream cheese and mix it in using a spoon. Chill the icing in the fridge for 10 minutes before using, to allow it to firm up a little.

Cut the cooled cake horizontally into 2 equal layers, but be careful, as the pineapple and pecans can tear the cake. Put one cake layer on a cake stand or plate. Spread a layer of cream cheese icing over the cake. Place the remaining layer of cake on top and spread the rest of the icing all over the cake with a spatula. Cover the bottom half of the outside of the cake with crushed pecans.

Lemon polenta cake

Polenta gives cakes a wonderful yellow colour with a pleasing grainy texture, while lemon juice and zest act as a counterpoint to the dense, buttery flavour of this cake.

2 large lemons

220 g/2 sticks salted butter, softened

220 g/1 cup plus 2 tablespoons caster/granulated sugar

4 eggs, lightly beaten

190 g/1⅓ cups ground almonds

125 g/1 cup polenta/cornmeal

1½ teaspoons baking powder

a 18-cm/7-inch round cake pan, baselined with parchment paper

SERVES 8

Preheat the oven to 150°C fan/ 170°C/325°F/Gas 3.

Grate the zest from both lemons, and squeeze the juice from just one.

In a large bowl, cream the butter and sugar together until pale and fluffy. Add the eggs one at a time, beating between each addition, then stir in the lemon juice and zest, followed by the ground almonds, polenta/cornmeal and baking powder.

Spoon the mixture into the prepared cake pan, smooth level with a palette knife and bake in the oven for 80–90 minutes. A skewer inserted in the middle should come out clean.

Remove from the oven and allow to stand for a while. When cool enough to handle, run a knife around the inside of the pan and turn out onto a wire rack to cool completely.

The cake will keep for 4–5 days in an airtight container.

Butter-glazed lemon cake

This easy teatime treat is finished with a tangy lemony butter glaze, which soaks deliciously into the cake.

200 g/1¾ sticks butter, softened

300 g/2½ cups caster/granulated sugar

a pinch of salt

3 eggs, beaten

320 g/2½ cups plain/all-purpose flour

1 teaspoon baking powder

200 ml/¾ cup plain yogurt

grated zest of 2 lemons

freshly squeezed juice of 1 lemon

BUTTER GLAZE

30 g/2 tablespoons butter

a pinch of salt

50 g/¼ cup caster/granulated sugar

freshly squeezed juice of 1 lemon

a 900-g/2-lb. loaf pan, lightly greased and lined with parchment paper

SERVES 8–10

Preheat the oven to 160°C fan/180°C/350°F/Gas 4.

Beat the butter, sugar and salt together until light and smooth. Add the beaten eggs a little at a time, until fully incorporated. If the mixture starts to curdle, simply add a little of the flour and stir in.

Add the remaining flour and baking powder, and stir well. Stir in the yogurt, and then the lemon zest and juice. Spoon the mixture into the prepared pan.

Bake in the preheated oven for about 1 hour 10 minutes, until golden and risen. A skewer inserted into the centre of the cake should come out clean.

Meanwhile, make the glaze. Put the butter, salt, sugar and lemon juice into a small saucepan and heat for 3–4 minutes until the sugar has dissolved and the mixture is syrupy. Pour over the hot cake. Leave the cake to cool in the pan for 15 minutes or so, then turn onto a wire rack to cool completely.

Fruit bread

*This traditional favourite is so simple to make and makes
a delicious teatime treat that actually tastes better a day or two
after baking. Serve thickly spread with butter.*

---

35 g/2½ tablespoons salted butter,
softened

65 g/⅓ cup packed dark brown sugar

1 egg

1 tablespoon black treacle/dark
molasses

165 g/1⅓ cups self-raising/rising
flour

a pinch of salt

¼ teaspoon mixed spice/apple
pie spice

¼ teaspoon ground cinnamon

65 g/½ cup sultanas/golden raisins

25 g/3 tablespoons chopped pecans

a 450-g/1-lb. loaf pan, lined with
parchment paper

SERVES ABOUT 8

Preheat the oven to 150°C fan/
170°C/325°F/Gas 3.

In a large bowl, cream the butter
and sugar together until pale and
fluffy. Add the egg and beat in.

In a separate bowl, combine
90 ml/6 tablespoons warm water
and the treacle/molasses, then add
to the creamed butter and stir to
mix. Sift together the flour, salt
and spices. Add to the bowl,
followed by the sultanas/golden
raisins and pecans, and beat to
a smooth mixture.

Spoon the mixture into the
prepared loaf pan and bake in the
preheated oven for 40–45 minutes
or until the top springs back with
light finger pressure or a skewer
inserted into the middle of the loaf
comes out clean.

The bread is best stored overnight
and then served spread with
butter. It will keep for up to 5 days
in an airtight container. It is
equally delicious when toasted.

Lavender loaf cake

Lavender has been used in baking for centuries and it takes just a tiny amount to add a delicate flavour to this simple cake.

---

130 g/1 stick plus 2 teaspoons salted butter, softened

130 g/⅔ cup caster/granulated sugar

2 eggs

grated zest of 1 lemon

35 g/3 tablespoons ground almonds

100 g/¾ cup plain/all-purpose flour

40 g/⅓ cup self-raising/rising flour

3 teaspoons dried lavender flowers (see Tip below)

a 450-g/1-lb. loaf pan, lined with parchment paper

SERVES ABOUT 8

Preheat the oven to 150°C fan/170°C/325°F/Gas 3.

In a large bowl, cream the butter and sugar together until pale and fluffy. Add the eggs one at a time, beating between each addition. Add the lemon zest, ground almonds and flours and beat to a smooth batter. Finally, add the lavender and stir through.

Spoon the mixture into the prepared loaf pan, spread level and bake in the preheated oven for 40 minutes. A skewer inserted into the middle of the loaf should come out clean. Remove from the oven and leave to cool in the pan for 30 minutes before turning out onto a wire rack to cool completely.

This cake is best eaten on the day of baking, but will keep for up to 4 days in an airtight container or frozen for up to 2 months.

Tip: If using home-grown lavender, be sure to wash it thoroughly and dry in a low oven. Alternatively, you can buy it online.

Strawberries & cream roulade

There are only three ingredients in a classic roulade cake (plus the filling): flour, sugar and eggs. A Swiss roll can be a dry cake as no oils have been used in the baking, so compensate with juicy fresh fruit and indulge in a little extra cream.

FILLING

200 g/2 cups strawberries

freshly squeezed juice of $\frac{1}{2}$ lemon

30 g/2$\frac{1}{2}$ tablespoons caster/granulated sugar

150 ml/$\frac{2}{3}$ cup whipping cream

$\frac{1}{2}$ teaspoon vanilla extract

50 g/6 tablespoons icing/confectioners' sugar

CAKE

200 g/7 oz. eggs, lightly whisked with 150 g/$\frac{3}{4}$ cup caster/granulated sugar

1 teaspoon vanilla extract

150 g/generous 1 cup plain/all-purpose or sponge flour

TO DECORATE

icing/confectioners' sugar

fresh strawberries

a 45 x 30-cm/18 x 12-inch non-stick Swiss roll/jelly roll pan, lightly oiled and baselined with parchment paper

MAKES 1 ROULADE

Preheat the oven to 120°C fan/140°C/280°F/Gas 1.

For the filling, hull and finely chop the strawberries. Place them in a bowl and fold in the lemon juice and caster/granulated sugar. Leave for 30 minutes to bring out the flavour. Whip the cream, vanilla extract and icing/confectioners' sugar to a light, just setting, whipped cream. Chill.

For the cake, take the prepared Swiss roll/jelly roll pan, oil the top of the paper and lightly flour the paper and the sides. Place the whisked eggs and caster/granulated sugar in a bowl and mix for at least 10 minutes with a hand-held electric whisk or in a stand mixer until tripled in volume and thick and creamy. Add the vanilla extract and whisk.

Gently fold in the flour, one-third at a time, until just combined.

Pour the mixture into the prepared Swiss roll/jelly roll pan and use a spatula to spread to an even depth. Immediately place the pan into the preheated oven and bake for 12 minutes. Check the cake is cooked by touch; it should bounce back when lightly pressed. If it is soft or it 'crackles' when touched, put it back in the oven for a further 2 minutes, then check again.

Remove from the oven and leave to cool for 2 minutes. Cover a wire rack with a piece of oiled and floured parchment paper and, carefully, turn the cake out onto the rack. Leave the cake to cool for 5 minutes.

While the cake is still a little warm, carefully peel the parchment paper off. Gently cut halfway through the cake, across the width of the cake, on the short side, about 1 cm/$\frac{1}{2}$ inch from the edge, this will help it roll up.

Starting from the side where you have made the cut, carefully roll up the cake and gently squeeze it to form the roll, before unrolling again in order to assemble the final cake.

Finish the filling by folding together the whipped cream and strawberries. Plaster the mixture generously onto the cake, then carefully roll up to make a roulade. Trim the ends off to make a neat finish and dust with icing/confectioners' sugar.

Green tea cream tart with strawberries & white chocolate

Use a good-quality green tea (matcha) as this determines the taste of the end result. A lovely matcha will have grassy, sweet notes that pair perfectly with the strawberries and white chocolate.

2 punnets of ripe strawberries
Green Tea Ganache (see page 141)
1 blind-baked Pâte Sablée pie crust
  (see page 133)

TO DECORATE
70 g/2½ oz. strawberry jam/preserve
1 tablespoon water
white chocolate, melted,
  for drizzling

SERVES 8–10

Hull some of the strawberries and leave the prettiest stalks on the others.

Spoon the Green Tea Ganache into the blind-baked pâte sablée pie crust and level with a spatula. Scatter the strawberries over the top in a decorative fashion, as you wish.

To make a glaze, put the strawberry jam and water in a small saucepan and bring to the boil, so that the jam is thin and hot. Brush or pour the glaze all over the strawberries, especially the cut tops.

Drizzle melted white chocolate all over the strawberries to decorate.

Tip: If you wish to prepare the tart a day in advance, brush the base of the blind-baked pie crust with melted white chocolate before adding the pastry cream, so that the crust doesn't get soggy while it sits in the fridge.

Hazelnut, peach & redcurrant frangipane tart

Hazelnut makes a lovely frangipane-style base for this peach and redcurrant-topped tart (vary the fruit according to season).

PASTRY

175 g/1½ sticks butter

50 g/¼ cup caster/granulated sugar

a pinch of salt

1 egg yolk

250 g/2 cups plain/all-purpose flour, plus extra for dusting

FILLING

200 g/1¾ sticks butter, softened

200 g/1⅓ cups toasted hazelnuts, finely chopped

200 g/1 cup caster/granulated sugar

a pinch of salt

2 eggs

6 ripe peaches, pitted/stoned and each one cut into 8 slices

150 g/generous 1 cup redcurrants

100 ml/6 tablespoons apricot jam/jelly, sieved

a 23-cm/9-inch tart pan with removable base

SERVES 8

Preheat the oven to 150°C fan/170°C/325°F/Gas 3.

To make the pastry, beat the butter, sugar and salt together until smooth. Add the egg yolk and stir until combined. Fold in the flour and bring the mixture together to form a smooth dough. Wrap in clingfilm/plastic wrap and leave to rest in a cool place while preparing the filling.

Beat the butter, hazelnuts, sugar, salt and eggs together until smooth. Roll the pastry out on a lightly floured surface and line the tart pan. Spoon the hazelnut filling evenly into the base. Bake in the preheated oven for about 30 minutes, until the filling is firm in the centre.

Arrange the sliced peaches over the top of tart in slightly overlapping concentric circles, starting at the outside edge. Scatter over the redcurrants. Warm the apricot jam/jelly slightly and stir in 1 tablespoon hot water. Brush it carefully over the top to glaze. Leave to cool.

Baked lemon ricotta tart

*This lovely, light baked ricotta tart works exceptionally well
served with a cup of delicately refreshing lemon verbena tea.*

⊰ — • • • — ⊱

PASTRY

175 g/1½ sticks butter, softened

50 g/¼ cup caster/granulated sugar

1 egg yolk

250 g/2 cups plain/all-purpose flour

FILLING

250 ml/1 cup double/heavy cream

500 g/2 cups ricotta

200 g/1 cup caster/granulated sugar

3 eggs, beaten

grated zest and juice of 2 large
lemons

icing/confectioners' sugar,
for dusting

a 23-cm/9-inch tart pan with
removable base

SERVES 8

To make the pastry, beat the butter
and sugar together until light and
fluffy. Add the egg yolk and beat
until smooth. Add the flour and
work the mixture lightly until it
forms a dough. Wrap the dough in
clingfilm/plastic wrap and leave to
rest in a cool place for 30 minutes.

Preheat the oven to 160°C fan/
180°C/350°F/Gas 4. Roll the
dough out to fit the tart pan on a
lightly floured surface. Chill while
preparing the filling.

To make the filling, beat the cream,
ricotta, sugar and eggs together
until smooth. Add the lemon zest
and juice and beat again.

Remove the pastry case from the
freezer and bake in the preheated
oven for 10 minutes, until firm.
Remove from the oven and pour
in the filling. Reduce the oven to
130°C fan/150°C/300°F/Gas 2
and bake for 45 minutes or until
the filling has set. Leave to cool
in the pan. Dust with icing/
confectioners' sugar and serve.

Menu planners

Here you will find a selection of themed menu planners to get you started. Each features suggestions for a selection of sandwiches, savouries, cakes and small fancies. Choose several from each menu and you can be sure they will complement each other, or prepare the entire spread if you really want to push the boat out for an extra special occasion.

TRADITIONAL AFTERNOON TEA

A selection of finger sandwiches
(page 35)

•

Plain scones (page 50)

•

Fruited Scones (page 52)

•

Raspberry macarons (page 147)

•

Blackcurrant millefeuilles
(page 108)

•

Lemon & lime meringue tartlets
(page 133)

•

Victoria Sandwich (page 158)

AN ELEGANT PARISIAN TEA

Crab mayonnaise éclairs (page 46)

•

Baby rarebits with beetroot
& orange relish (page 43)

•

Bijous blondies (page 86)

•

Fraises-des-bois friands (page 70)

•

Cherry crumble Paris-Brests
(page 121)

•

Tea voyage macarons (page 141)

•

Butter-glazed lemon cake
(page 170)

A GARDEN PARTY TEA
FOR SUMMER

Cucumber & mint sandwiches
(page 24)

•

Coronation chicken sandwiches
(page 31)

•

Ham & mustard sandwiches
(page 33)

•

Peach melba scones (page 61)

•

Mini madeleines with a citrus
posset (page 74)

•

Raspberry & clotted cream whirls
(page 77)

•

Hummingbird cake (page 165)

•

Green tea tart with strawberries
& white chocolate (page 179)

A FIRESIDE TEA
FOR WINTER

Aubergine/eggplant & mayonnaise
sandwiches (page 26)

•

Beef & horseradish sandwiches
(page 28)

•

Welsh rarebit (page 36)

•

Olive & anchovy whirls (page 44)

•

Apple & cinnamon scones
(page 55)

•

Orange & cranberry Scones
(page 56)

•

Praline & coffee éclairs (page 130)

•

Fruit bread (page 173)

A ROMANTIC TEA FOR VALENTINE'S DAY

Smoked salmon & asparagus
crostini (page 40)

•

Rose cream religieuses (page 113)

•

Passion fruit éclairs (page 119)

•

Raspberry meringue kisses
(page 139)

•

Dark chocolate, prune
& Armagnac mousses (page 148)

•

Crème brûlée spoons (page 154)

A VINTAGE BIRTHDAY CELEBRATION

Egg & cress sandwiches (page 30)

•

Ham & mustard sandwiches
(page 33)

Raspberry brownies (page 84)

•

Rocky road slices (page 89)

•

Butterfly cakes (page 92)

•

Cherry bakewell cupcakes
(page 97)

•

Individual no-bake cookie butter
cheesecakes (page 150)

•

Strawberries & cream roulade
(page 177)

A FLORAL TEA FOR
MOTHER'S DAY

Smoked salmon & dill mayonnaise
sandwiches (page 25)

•

Hummus & rocket/arugula
sandwiches (page 27)

•

Cheese & rosemary scones
(page 62)

•

Lemon-basil cupcakes (page 99)

•

Rose thins (page 105)

•

Violet éclairs (page 123)

•

Lavender loaf cake (page 174)

A HIGH TEA FOR
FATHER'S DAY

Beef & horseradish sandwiches
(page 28)

•

Little toasts with anchovy butter
& quail's eggs (page 39)

•

Triple cheese scones with whipped
mustard butter (page 65)

•

Rhubarb & custard macarons
(page 143)

•

Black forest fondant fancies
(page 78)

•

Fruit cake (page 160)

Index

RECIPE CREDITS

Mickael Benichou
Bijoux blondies
Lemon-basil cupcakes
Pavlova cupcakes
Tea voyage macarons

Susannah Blake
Baby rarebits with beetroot/beet
  & orange relish
Dark chocolate, prune
  & Armagnac mousses
Finger sandwich selection
Little toasts with anchovy butter
  & quails' eggs
Praline & coffee éclairs
Smoked salmon & asparagus
  crostini
Walnut & orange scones

Julian Day
Butterfly cakes
Lavender loaf cake
Lemon cookies
Lemon polenta cake
Meringue nests
Shortbread

Matt Follas
Aubergine/eggplant & mayonnaise
  sandwiches
Beef & horseradish sandwiches
Coronation chicken sandwiches
Crème brûlée spoons
Cucumber & mint sandwiches
Egg & cress sandwiches
Fruit cake

Ham & mustard sandwiches
Hummus & rocket sandwiches
Lemon & lime meringue tartlets
Pink meringue kisses
Plain scones
Raspberry brownies
Rose thins
Smoked salmon & dill
  mayonnaise sandwiches
Strawberries & cream roulade
Victoria sandwich
Welsh rarebit

Liz Franklin
Almond financiers
Apple & cinnamon scones
Baked lemon ricotta tart
Butter-glazed lemon cake
Clotted cream & raspberry brûlée
  tartlets
Frais-de-bois friands
Hazelnut, peach & redcurrant
  frangipane tart
Introduction (pages 8–17)
Raspberry & clotted cream whirls
Raspberry macarons
Vanilla butter cookies
Vegan brownies

Victoria Hall
Cheese & rosemary scones
Cherry bakewell cupcakes

Hannah Miles
Blackcurrant éclairs
Blackcurrant millefeuilles
Caramel Paris-Brests
Cherry crumble Paris-Brests
Choquettes
Mini madeleines with citrus posset
Passion fruit éclairs
Peach melba scones
Pistachio religieuses
Rocky road slices
Rose cream religieuses
Violet éclairs
White chocolate & raspberry
  cheesecake bites

Suzy Pelta
Individual no-bake cookie
  butter cheesecakes

Will Torrent
Black Forest fondant fancies
Crab mayonnaise éclairs
Fruited scones
Mango & coconut millefeuilles
Olive & anchovy whirls
Rhubarb & custard macarons
Triple cheese scones with
  whipped mustard butter

Bea Vo
Apple bourbon pecan cake
Green tea cream tart with
  strawberries & white chocolate
Hummingbird cake
Orange & cranberry scones

PHOTOGRAPHY CREDITS

Martin Brigdale
Pages 23, 35, 38, 41, 42, 49,
59, 131 & 149.

David Brittain
Page 21.

Adrian Lawrence
Pages 63, 96 & 151.

William Lingwood
Pages 1, 60, 69, 75, 88, 109
& 152.

Steve Painter
Pages 2, 22, 26, 29, 32, 37,
51, 68, 85, 87, 91, 93, 95,
99, 103, 104, 107, 134, 138,
139, 142, 157, 159, 161, 168,
172, 175 & 176 & 177.

Matt Russell
Pages 7, 45, 47, 48, 53, 67,
79, 111 & 145.

Kate Whitaker
Pages 3, 5, 31, 57, 105, 106,
112, 114, 115, 116, 118, 122,
124, 126, 127, 128, 140, 156,
162, 165, 167, 179 & 192.

Isobel Wield
Pages 4, 8, 12, 13, 14, 15, 16,
18, 19, 20, 25, 33, 54, 64,
71, 72, 76, 82, 83, 100, 130,
132, 147, 17, 181 & 182.